MOUNTAIN MYSTERIES

Marvin Gregory and P. David Smith

PRESS

Published by Wayfinder Press
P.O. Box 217
Ridgway, Colorado 81432

Typesetting - The Silverton Standard and The Miner
           Silverton, Colorado
Printing - Publishers Press
           Salt Lake City, Utah

Cover art - Clarke Cohu
Cover Photos - Bill Fries III
Cartography - Anvil Mountain Graphics

FOREWORD

The forerunner of this book was originally published in 1981 by the Ouray County Chamber of Commerce. The original manuscript had been written by P. David Smith and then revised and extensively supplemented by Waldo Butler who died shortly before the book was complete. Since that time, several inaccuracies have been noted. Some of the jeep and hiking trails have been improved or have deteriorated. In early 1984, Marvin Gregory and P. David Smith undertook a major revision of the original text. Many thanks to Jan and Tricia Smith for their help in typing the revised manuscript. Extensive new written material has been added as well as many historic photographs. All of the book's maps have been extensively revised. Publication of the book was taken over by Wayfinder Press.

At one time or another, all of us have fallen victim to some of the extravagances, exaggerations and misconceptions that have crept into so many written accounts about the local history. The telling of the story by some writers, the retelling by others (often with added embellishments), further misinterpretations and some deliberate hoaxes can lead to a very confusing, questionable accounting of history. Logical reasoning and research into reliable, believable sources (i.e. public records) simply will not support many of these accounts.

An attempt is being made in this book to winnow some of the "chaff" from the "grain." We will not tell you, for example, that Tom Walsh "bought the Hope Diamond" for his wife or his daughter, for he did not buy it at all! We will not tell you that one of our now extinct "ghost towns" once had "ten thousand residents," for census records show that ten thousand people have never lived in Ouray County at any one time. We will not tell you that "Mt. Sneffels is Colorado's richest mountain, honeycombed with mines, villages built on its slopes, etc.," for none of this is true. If there are rich ore veins on, in or under Mount Sneffels, nobody has found them yet.

Ouray County's history needs no embellishment to make it interesting reading. We cannot guarantee that NO ERRORS are in this book, but insofar as possible, we hope to offer you true, believable history such as can be supported by documentable evidence.

P. David Smith
Marvin Gregory
Ouray, Colorado
May 1987

WARNING

These mountains can be dangerous. Always use common sense. Conditions may have changed between the time this book was written and the time you are using it. Make sure you have adequate provisions and up to date directions. If hiking, give your body a few days to adjust to the high altitude and avoid hypothermia by wearing warm clothes and taking enough food and water. If you get lost, stop, keep warm and don't panic. If you can't figure your way out, stay put and don't try to hike out. If you build a fire, make sure to clear the area and dig a pit. Forest fires are an ever present danger. Always try to let people know where you will be and when you will return. When driving, always stay on your side of the road and gear your vehicle down so you won't wear out your brakes. Don't try slopes that are too steep and keep on the road. Above all admit your limitations. Whether walking, climbing or jeeping remember that it always looks easier going up than coming down. These warnings are to point out the dangers that go with the pleasures. Nothing can compare to Ouray's fresh air, clean streams, beautiful scenery and nights of sparkling stars. Enjoy yourself.

Table of Contents

Magnificent, photogenic, 12,800-foot-high Mount Abrams stands guard over the spectacular Uncompahgre Gorge and the narrow portion of the Uncompahgre Valley, in which is situated the "Gem City of the Rockies," Ouray. Within the scope of this picture, more eons of earth's history become an "open book" than at any other place on the North American continent. (Bob Petley-Courtesy Ouray County Chamber of Commerce)

INTRODUCTION

"Ouray is - what shall I say? The prettiest mountain town in Colorado? That wouldn't do. A dozen other places would deny it ... Yet that it is among the most attractive in situation, in climate, in appearance, and in the society it affords, there can be no doubt. There are few western villages that can boast so much civilization."

Ernest Ingersoll - 1885

And now, over a hundred years later, things haven't changed much. Civilization - that is the word for it - not to be found in the steel, glass and asphalt of the city, but rather in the streams, flowers and mountains of Ouray.

It takes a long time to see Ouray County. Most of the enjoyment has to be fought for - either in a four-wheel-drive Jeep or gasping for every breath on the high mountain trails. Within a dozen miles the topography changes from the pinon and scrub oak hills of the Colona area (elevation 6,300 feet), to the high green meadows of Cow Creek, to the rough and rugged peaks of Mount Sneffels (elevation 14,150 feet). You can find what you are looking for in Ouray whether it's lake or river fishing; elk, deer or pheasant hunting; jeeping; mountain climbing; river rafting; cross country skiing; snowshoeing; gold panning; mineral collecting; hiking; snowmobiling; backpacking; birdwatching; or any of a dozen other sports. The "Switzerland of America" offers it all. The main attraction, however, is that the area abounds in history. Everywhere there are relics of the old mining days - cabins, boilers, tunnels and whole ghost towns. What, therefore, makes Ouray so unique is that sports, history and the joy of being outdoors in some of the most beautiful scenery in the world can all be entwined.

The old ghost towns and mines abound in Ouray, but year by year nature takes its toll. Heavy snows probably do the most damage. Man takes his toll - tearing down some structures for the wood and just vandalizing others. Most of the mining camps in Ouray that were abandoned more than fifty years ago are now no more than mounds of dirt. Many of the newer structures are only piles of rubble. All of this helps to remind one of just how small man's achievements really are and how easily they can be forgotten.

From the time of its discovery, the Ouray area has fascinated, awed and inspired all who have entered the area. The Rev. J.J. Gibbons, a local early day priest, wrote in his book, **In The San Juans**, 1898:

"No man can travel through the mountains without a deepening impression of the majesty of The Creator; no one can stand in the presence of the snow-capped peaks, over which sunshine and shadow pursue each other, without feeling an impulse to elevate his soul to God, the author and finisher of the beautiful and the sublime. A trip to the mountains convinces the religious mind of the existence of a divine power, wisdom and goodness, and inspires men of good will with the resolution to seek first the kingdom of God and His justice. Where all is so divine, surely the spirit of man should not be merely human.''

At night as well as day the area is enchanting. Ernest Ingersoll, a travel writer for **Harper's Weekly**, in 1883 wrote while on horseback near Ouray:

"The air was cool and soft and drowsy. The stars shone with a brilliance which long ago suggested to the savage mind that they were pin-holes in the canopy through which beamed that ineffable refulgence of an endless day to be attained when the probation of this life was over. Every moment or two a meteor would leap out, flash with pale brilliance across the firmament, eclipsing the steady stars for an instant, and then disappear as though behind a veil.''

Not only has the man of God and the tourist been inspired by Ouray's beauty but also the scientist - even the geologist who many people today think of as joining in the rape of the land. C.L. Hall in **Mineral Resources of Ouray County** which was published in 1894 wrote:

"No greater diversity of natural resources did the Almighty ever plant on an equal area ... Perennial streams, as pure as crystal, come dancing down from the eternal snow-banks, and water and fertilize all the central valleys ... Men partake of the nature of the section of the country they inhabit and if here they become strong mentally and physically, as this region is rugged and grand, they will not be long dominated by the effete money kings and their political hirelings of the East.

"Ouray is peerless. She will be famous as a mountain resort when many of the now celebrated watering places are abandoned and forgotten. The flora of her mountain slopes is of great beauty and variety. Flowers adorn the mountains and make redolent the atmosphere ... Daisies, buttercups, the meek-eyed violet, beautiful columbines, the verbena and other delicate blossoms, abound above timberline and nestle in the very borders of the eternal snowdrifts ... Beauty and grandeur, and glory intermingle, and man stands appalled.''

Ouray County is basically mountainous with three main valleys and rivers - The Uncompahgre, The Dallas, and Cow Creek. The county is thirty miles long north to south and twenty-nine miles wide at the north, while tapering almost to a point at the south.

At almost any time of spring or summer, some part of Ouray County is going to be abundant with flowers. The growing season lasts for almost 125 days in the northern part of the county but is almost nonexistent high in the southern mountains. Almost every type of vegetation life zone that exists in Colorado is also present in Ouray. The desert and plains zones are the only zones missing. In Colorado the prevalent plant life is determined basically by altitude. Every 1,000 feet of elevation is similar to driving 350 miles north at sea level.

The foothills (lower Montane) are basically in the Colona to Ridgway area. Cottonwood, scrub oak, box elder, pinon, sage and juniper are

Streams, fed by the continuous melt of snowfields in the high San Juan basins, seem in a big hurry to get down to warmer climes. (Bill Fries III)

plentiful. Late fall hunting is best in this area. Spring comes here in April and May.

The next area is the Canadian or Montane zone found in the upper portions of the three major valleys. Pine, aspen and willows are the predominant trees. Flowers normally bloom in May to July. From 10,000 feet to timberline is the subalpine zone. Spruce and fir predominate. Trees usually grow in clumps and flowers bloom from June to August. Above timberline (11,500 feet), trees do not grow and the area is called arctic or alpine. Mosses, lichen and grasses predominate. This is an extremely fragile and delicate area so **please stay on the traveled paths!**

The San Juan Mountains that run through southern Ouray County create the largest and the most mineralized range in Colorado and cover about 12,000 square miles. They are also the newest from a geologic point of view which also helps to make them the steepest. They thus have the nickname "The Switzerland of America." Twice (a billion years ago and 600 million years ago) mountains have been formed in the area and then worn down to nothing by erosion. Most of the current mountains in the San Juans were formed 20 to 75 million years ago, largely by lava and ash from volcanoes with the subsequent valleys and canyons being formed by glacial, water and wind erosion. Most of the minerals were deposited during the volcanic activity of this time. However, not only were the mountains building up, but the valleys and canyons were being worn down. In about 12 million more years the mountains will be flat again!

High above timberline in the San Juans, we may see great cirques where glaciers were, geologically speaking, not so very long ago. The gentler slopes overlain with "tundra," a very rich, productive soil, capable of producing good grass and many Alpine plants and flowers, some of it as thin as two inches requiring thousands of years to build. Tundra, if not destroyed by man's exploitation, is capable of storing more water, delivering it as needed for man's use, than all the reservoirs built by men. (Bill Fries III)

In early times, some mines were opened and operated by their discoverers with little capital. Such would seem to be the case with the mine pictured here. These "miners" do not appear to be properly dressed for going "down in the mine," nor does the ore car appear to be loaded with ordinary "muck." (Denver Public Library)

Nineteen layers of rock formations can be found in the Ouray area. Because the layers of the earth's crust are tilted, there is almost 26,000 feet of the earth's crust visible. Generally speaking, the ores in the San Juan area were formed when mineralized water and gas solutions were forced upwards from deep in the earth into the softer rock and through cracks and crevices. Here, it cooled around the harder rock. The resulting mineralized zones are therefore called fissure lodes. The Ouray deposits are generally grouped as silver-bearing fissure veins, gold-bearing fissure veins, replacement deposits in quartzite and replacement deposits in limestone. The veins are usually wide and have well defined walls or sides. The usual minerals found in the Ouray area include native gold, gold-bearing pyrite, tetrahedrite, chalcopyrite, argentiferous galena, ruby silver and brittle silver. The upheaval stopped about three million years ago. Then for centuries water has rushed over the exposed portions of veins carrying small parts of the gold or other mineral downstream and exposing other veins. The most frequent ore in Ouray is galena—a lead and silver ore which frequently contains gray copper. As a general rule ore gets richer the higher up in the mountains that it is found because of the cooling process.

A few mining terms will be helpful: A crosscut is a tunnel that comes into a vein from an angle; an adit is an horizontal mine entrance. A raise is an opening going up; shafts and winzes go down.　The cavity of considerable dimension after ore is removed is a stope. Skips are the "elevators" that go up and down the shafts (most don't go up and down but rather at an angle). Gangue or matrix is the worthless rock dug out but contain ore and cannot be separated from it at the mine. Country rock is also worthless and is left in dumps outside the mine. A very complete description of the different types of mining in 1880 in Colorado can be found in Frank Fossett's book **Colorado, Its Gold and Silver Mines**. In reading this book, gold and silver will be reported in terms of both money and weight. Mining lode claims in Ouray cover a little more than 10 acres (10.33 to be exact) and are generally 300 feet wide by 1500 feet long. Placer claims were 20 acres maximum although 2 or more claims could be combined up to 160 acres. Claims are either patented (owned outright by a private individual) or unpatented (which requires the locator to do annual work on the property until he gets his patent or loses it). Silver and gold production was given in ounces and by amount. To convert older production figures one can figure $1.00 to $1.20 for silver and $16 to $20 for gold (although the exact figures vary according to the exact time and purity, and at the mill the miner might get only 50 to 60% of this).

Some idea of mining and the equipment used should help increase the enjoyment of what you are seeing in the Ouray area. It might also help in collecting minerals. Prospectors first looked for gold or silver. The two are almost always found together although there may only be minute quantities of one or the other. The accepted method was to placer, which is washing the suspected gravel in pans, flumes or sluice boxes. "Panning" will still pick up traces of gold and silver in Ouray's streams. The heavier minerals sink to the bottom and the dirt washes away. The term placer (pronounced plasser) is derived from the Spanish "Plazo de oro" or "place of gold." Silver is not normally found by the amateur in placering as the mineral turns green-black, grey, or brown when exposed to the elements. Care should be taken not to confuse gold with the more prevalent pyrite which is brittle, more copper-colored and usually in cubes. Gold is dull, malleable and will look the same color from all directions. Many other species of rock can be found. Over 445 types of rocks have been found in Colorado and eventually most can be found in Ouray. Be careful not to prospect on private property. If you plan to do much work at all you should become familiar with state and federal mining laws.

Early miners followed "float" back to the vein where samples were taken and brought to the assay offices to determine its content. If warranted, a shaft was driven; but if possible, a tunnel was better as it needed no hoist with its attendant buckets and steam engines. Tunnels were also better for draining water from the mines by gravity rather than by pumps. As the ore came out of the mines it was sorted and stored above chutes to await transportation by burro, wagon or aerial tram. The simplest trams were run by gravity with the heavily loaded tram going down pulling the empty one up. Crushing or stamp mills crudely recovered the minerals by pulverizing the ore with heavy weights (stamps) and running the powder over copper-plated tables coated with mercury to attract gold and silver. If the ore had a high lead content a better method was to use the harsh blast furnaces of the smelters to separate the precious metals.

The climate of Ouray has never been harsh. Rarely does the temperature of Ouray go below zero in the winter and 40-degree days are common. Snow is light and dry but abundant. Wind is usually non-existent in Ouray except during severe storms and sometimes in the spring. Summers are usually cool with highs in the 70's and 80's and lows in the 50's or 60's. Almost daily, rains fall in July and August, but the autumn is usually dry with warm days and chilly nights. The low humidity and lack of wind always make it seem warmer than it actually is. This fact leads many to go into the mountains unprepared. Hypothermia (lowering of the body's core temperature) can happen even in the summer at high altitudes. The wetness and wind of summer thunderstorms can severely lower body temperature. To avoid hypothermia, wear warm clothes; take rain gear, snacks and water; and try to avoid exhaustion. Another danger of thunderstorms is lightning. Stay off high points during a storm, don't huddle together and stay in your vehicle if you have one.

Wildlife in Ouray includes chipmunks (they will eat out of your hand at Box Canyon Park), marmots or "whistle pigs" (they look like large groundhogs), ptarmigan, squirrels, beaver, skunks, porcupines, rabbits, bobcats, deer, elk, and mountain sheep. Less frequently seen are black bear, mountain lions, wolves and coyotes. Deer and elk are seen mostly in early morning and at dusk. In the summer they inhabit the high grassy meadows, but as winter approaches the herds move to lower elevations. They can commonly be seen alongside (and sometimes in) the road during the winter. When hunting please be sure that you are on public land or have the permission of the owner. Pay close attention to weather reports in the fall. Remember the road you came in on may be impassible after a heavy snowfall.

Many bird species are found including swallows, magpies, robins, bluebirds, jays, sparrows, eagles (mainly golden), hawks, grouse, pheasant, quail, doves, ducks and owls. Also, hummingbirds feed from bright feeders throughout Ouray in the warmer months. Trout are either native or stocked in most of the streams except the higher (southern) Uncompahgre which runs too cloudy. Varieties of trout in our area include cutthroat, rainbow, brook and some brown trout. Many of the high altitude lakes have good fishing. Some areas are limited to artificial lures and flies and other areas are posted. Spring runoff normally makes fishing poor and dangerous in May and June.

No variety of poisonous snake is known to exist in Ouray and only a few garden-type snakes are found. However, in May and June, you should look out for the tick (which can carry Rocky Mountain fever).

Four-wheeling and motorcycling have long been favorite sports in the Ouray area which is known to some as the "Jeep Capital of the World." Today's jeep roads are generally the old mining roads of the past. When driving in the mountains (whether on good roads or four-wheel-drive) remember a few safety tips. Snow may be on the roads even in July or August. Drifts and mud make roads slick. Always stay on your side of the road no matter how steep the dropoff to your side. Look ahead not down. Gear down on downgrades so you won't burn out your brakes. Remember the car going **up** grade has the right-of-way on one-lane roads. Drive only on the road so you do not damage the very fragile soil (especially in the high country where it may take tundra a hundred years to repair itself). Be careful where you stop and if you do on an incline, block your wheels.

Be careful when hiking or camping. Every year many parties get lost or hurt in the Ouray area. Make sure you have adequate provisions and directions or maps. Be careful to adjust your body for a few days to the high altitude. At 10,000 feet there is only half as much oxygen in the air as at sea level. Try not to hike or jeep alone. Wear warm clothing and take rain gear and plenty of water (the high altitude burns it out of your body much quicker than at low altitude). Always try to let someone know where you are going. If you get lost, stop, keep warm and don't panic. If

The marvelous jeep has made it possible to visit some of the world's most magnificent scenery coupled with a lot of history, if one is so inclined. Before the advent of the jeep, these places were accessible to a comparative few. (Bill Fries III)

The Sneffels Range. Her majesty, Mount Sneffels and members of her court; Whitehouse Mountain, Potosi, Teakettle Mountain, Gilpin—beautiful and friendly when treated with proper respect; when not, their "justice" can be swift and terrible! (Bill Fries III)

you can't figure your way out, stay put and someone will come for you. Always try to build some sort of signal.

Please pack out your trash and "leave only footprints - take only photos." Remember that most mines and the buildings and tools on them are private property. Be careful with your fires - make sure that they are out before moving on.

Don't try slopes that are too steep. It always looks easier going up than coming down. Much of the San Juan area is covered with loose rock that can be kicked down on your companions, so be careful and stay close together.

Cross country skiing, snowshoeing and snowmobiling are favorite wintertime activities in Ouray. In most cases, jeep roads, which in winter are impassible to vehicles, make excellent trails for these sports but be careful of avalanches. Be familiar with basic winter safety essentials. Snow cover is generally deep enough for these sports by November and snow lasts until late April or early May. East Dallas and Owl Creek Pass Road are especially good for these sports.

As a final warning, please remember that these mountains can be dangerous! Always use common sense. Conditions may have changed between the time this book was written and the time you are using it. Know and admit your limitations. These warnings are merely to point out the dangers that go with Ouray's many pleasures. Nothing can compare to Ouray's fresh air, clean streams, beautiful scenery and nights of sparkling stars. Enjoy yourself in Ouray's "Civilization."

CHAPTER 1
The San Juans
The First 35,000,000 Years

Fire and ice shaped these mountains and created one of the most spectacular landscapes in the world. It was to be called the "Roof of the Continent," a "Mountain Wonderland," and the "Gem of the Rockies." Nature also blessed the area with deposits of metallic ores which were richer than even the dreams of the early Spanish explorers who had penetrated the American Southwest in search of the legendary seven cities of gold.

About 35 million years ago, during the time geologists call the Oligocene epoch, global changes created a series of volcanic eruptions. Over the next five million years there was a outpouring of 8,000 cubic miles of lava across what is now the San Juans. Great craters were formed near present-day Silverton, Lake City and Creede. Immense internal pressures fractured the earth in thousands of places. Mineral solutions flowed upwards into these openings and were deposited as various ores when they neared the surface. Then, during the last two million years, ice deposits formed which eventually became thousands of feet thick and reached to the tops of all but the highest summits. Through incessant movement the glaciers scoured the valleys to their present shapes and carved the amphitheatres and needle-shaped peaks. Then, following the retreat of glaciers about 10,000 years ago, the steep slopes were subject to numerous landslides. The glaciers and the slides were to expose the mountains' riches to the men who appeared on the scene only a little more than a hundred years ago.

In the last century, the 50 mining districts that comprise the 12,000 square miles of the San Juan region have produced over $735 million in gold, silver, copper, lead, zinc and other precious metals. These minerals would be worth billions on today's market. Just west of the San Juans are deposits of carnotite that have yielded additional millions in uranium, vanadium and radium. Geologists believe that large quantities of gold, silver and other precious minerals still exist in the San Juans. To the north and south on the Colorado plateau lie huge untapped deposits of coal, oil shale and natural gas. Most hardrock mines, however, have closed due to the high price of production rather than a lack of ore.

The Utes were probably the first men to travel very far into the San Juans. Although the Anasazi (or Ancient Ones) occupied the Mesa Verde area to the south of the San Juans as early as 1 A. D. and man also occupied small caves near the Delta area at least 3,000 years ago, it is unlikely (and no signs have been found) that they often ventured into the mountains. About the year 1300, the Utes were forced into the mountains by the stronger, more populous Plains Indians. They soon roamed from present-day central New Mexico to Wyoming and from the front range of

Logging trains carrying timbers for Virginius Mine at 12,500 feet. Stony Mountain, prominent in the background, is a volcanic "plug"—softer materials have been removed from around it by glacial action and natural erosion processes. Some of the neighboring mountains are composed of volcanic "tuff" rather than lava or magma. (Ruth Gregory Collection)

Colorado into eastern Utah. At no time did the entire Ute Nation ever number more than three or four thousand. They generally broke into small family groups of several dozen or less that would winter in the lower valleys and then range back up into the mountains in the summer in search of game. In the mid-17th century the Utes obtained the horse from the Spaniards and their range increased. They began to alternately make war and peace with the Apaches - sometimes intermarrying and always willing to wage war against a common enemy such as the hated Comanche.

Although Spain claimed the local area since Coronado's time (1546), it was not until the late 18th century that the Spaniards began to explore Southwest Colorado. Juan Maria de Rivera came through the area in 1765. He passed near Delta where he carved his initials, a cross and the date in a young poplar tree. Most of the rivers and mountains had already been given Spanish names by the time that the Dominguez-Escalante expedition came through the area in 1776, soon after the signers of the Declaration of Independence had met in Philadelphia. They called the Utes the "Yuta" and the party came over the Dallas Divide-Log Hill area in late summer. Escalante wrote that the purpose of the expedition was to "open up a route by northern latitudes from Santa Fe to Monterey, California, with an eye to the conversion of tribes north and west of the Colorado River." When he reached the present-day site of Delta, Escalante found Rivera's initials carved in the poplar tree. A map published by Humboldt in 1811 referred to what is now the San Juans as the "Sierra de las Guillas," and a few other early-day trappers and geographers wrote generally about the area in the early 1800's.

Colorado statehood was difficult in coming. After the U. S. war with Mexico in 1848, the area became a possession of the United States.

Many animal-skin teepees of the Utes near the first Los Pinos Agency in the Cochetopa region. They are waiting for "issue day," when the agency will dole out flour, dried fruit, blankets, etc. and will turn cattle loose, one or two at a time, which the Indians will run down and kill in the manner of hunting buffalo. (Colorado Historical Society)

From 1851 until 1861, it was part of the Utah Territory. Statehood first died in committee in 1863 and in 1864, Colorado citizens voted U. S. statehood down. In 1865 and 1867 statehood was accepted by Colorado citizens but vetoed. Again, in 1872, statehood for Colorado and New Mexico was lost. Finally, in the centennial year of 1876, Colorado received what it had been striving for and became the 38th state.

Antoine Robideaux, St. Louis born and of a large French family, came west in 1824, hoping to make his fortune in the fur trade. Beaver hats were high fashion at that time and, of course, the fiber needed for their manufacture was obtained from beaver pelts. He arrived at Santa Fe where he remained for some four years, marrying a local senorita and becoming a citizen of the Republic of Mexico. In 1828, he made his way into the Uncompahgre Valley where he established "Fort Robideaux" (some writers have also called it "Fort Uncompahgre") near the place where the Uncompahgre River joins the Gunnison River north of the San Juans.

The enterprise was never very successful, perhaps partly because he did little or no trading with the Indians as was the case with most trading posts of the time; rather, his business was limited to supplying fur trappers and purchasing beaver pelts from them. Because of their proximity, it seems almost certain that fur trappers were in the nearby San Juans.

Robideaux did continue the fort's operation, however, until 1844. It was then that he realized that it had failed economically and appeared to have no future. To make matters worse, the Indians had become more and more hostile. After Robideaux had abandoned his "fort," the Indians in a symbolic gesture set fire to the buildings; however, there were some remains of the Fort when homesteaders settled the area following the removal of the Utes in 1881. Farmers, having no thought about future historic value, cleared away the remains, plowed the ground and planted crops.

In 1860, gold was discovered southeast of Silverton by Captain Charles Baker. There is a legend that in 1863, two prospectors made a rich gold strike in the Oak Creek area near Ouray but finally fled in fear of the Utes. In 1870, a party of prospectors was sent by Governor Pile of New Mexico to the Baker's Park area. They did placer mining in Arastra Gulch (originally called French Gulch after Adnah French, but later named after an arastra the prospectors found there.) Government officials reported that in 1871 there were 27 tons of ore taken from the Silverton area which yielded an average of $150 per ton. Most of this output came from a group working an outcropping on the Little Giant Vein which had been discovered by Miles T. Johnson in 1870. In 1871, George Howard, who had been with the original Baker group, built his cabin and founded Howardsville near the site of present-day Silverton.

In 1864, Robert Darling and a group of Mexican army officers prospected near present-day Rico. The San Juans were in the Ute Indian Reservation until 1873, but in that year, two-thirds of present-day Ouray and all of San Juan County were sold to the United States by the Utes. As soon as the San Juans were opened to mining (and perhaps before), it is likely that prospectors were at least in the southern end of Ouray County. It was not until 1875 that written history recorded that early miners found their way over the rugged San Juan Mountains to the area that is now Ouray County; however, the previous year, members of the Hayden U.S. Geographic and Geological Survey were in the area and had climbed Mt. Sneffels.

La Plata County Courthouse in Howardsville. Ouray was in La Plata County at the time of its founding, but by the time of Ouray's incorporation, San Juan County had been carved out of La Plata and the county seat had been moved to Silverton. Just over three months later, Ouray County was cut out of San Juan, leaving that county as it now appears on the maps. (Ruth Gregory Collection)

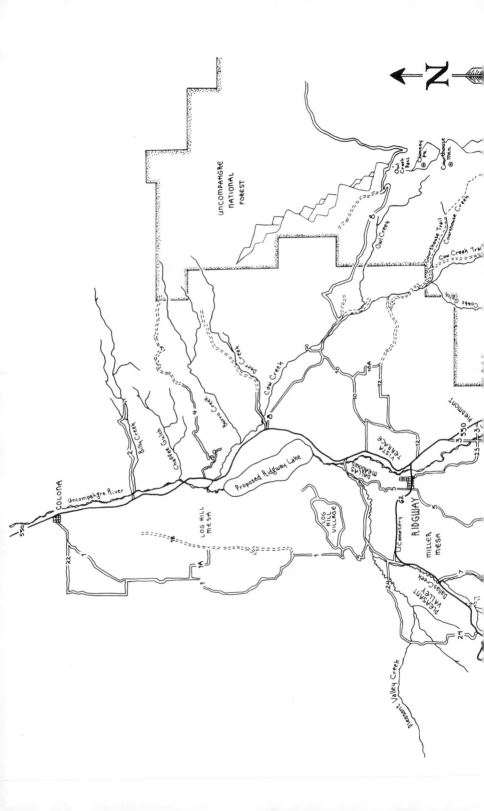

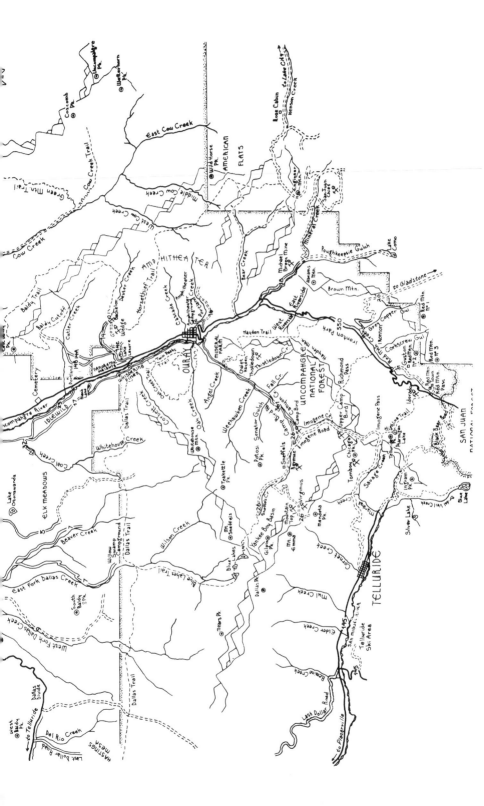

CHAPTER 2
Ouray County
The Utes Must Go

Early-day prospectors were high in the mountains near Engineer Mountain in the Mineral Point area by 1874. In 1875, large groups of men were making their way down the Uncompahgre River and Bear Creek. The first recorded entry into what is now the location of the City of Ouray is generally accepted to have occurred in July 1875 when A.W. "Gus" Begole and John Eckles entered the area from the Engineer Mountain - Bear Creek area. They made some promising discoveries and went back to Silverton for supplies. They returned with others and on August 11, 1875, Jacob Ohlwiler, Begole and John Morrow located the Cedar and Clipper claims within the present-day townsite. Eight other prospectors filed a declaration notice for the townsite of Uncompahgre on August 28, 1875.

It is sometimes written that Ouray was at first "called" Uncompahgre. That is not an accurate statement for the name never had popular use. The Town of Uncompahgre apparently "died a-borning." A probable explanation is that all Territorial and Federal officialdom were very much absorbed in preparing to make the transition from "Territory of Colorado" to full statehood. On February 10, 1874, La Plata County (containing most of present-day Ouray County as well as several future counties) was carved out of Lake and Conejos Counties. At the time of filing of the "Declaration Notice," Howardsville was the county seat of La Plata County. By January 31, 1876, San Juan County (comprised of present-day Ouray, San Juan, San Miguel and Dolores counties) had been carved out of La Plata County, Silverton becoming the seat of the new county. Therefore, by the time of the later filing for the townsite of Ouray, almost precisely two months after statehood for Colorado became official on August 1, 1876, the town of Ouray was incorporated by act of the commissioners of San Juan County, as empowered to do under the laws of the new State of Colorado. It is interesting that the plat of the town of Uncompahgre on 160 acres fits precisely on that portion of the larger (300-acre) plat of the town of Ouray. Even street, avenue, block and lot numbers are the same.

By August 23, 1875, A.J. Staley and Logan Whitlock had discovered the rich Fisherman and Trout lodes, located in present-day Box Canyon Park. Later that October, Begole and Eckles discovered the even richer Mineral Farm Mine about a mile southwest of town. Log cabins were built, and a small group of men spent at least part of the winter working the area and establishing several more placer claims. Unknown to them, rich discoveries had been made that summer in Imogene and Yankee Boy basins southwest of town.

Earliest picture of Ouray that we can find is this pen-and-ink rendering, probably made during the first quarter of 1877 when snow was on the ground. It was during this period that Ouray County was carved out of San Juan County and the town of Ouray became a county seat. (Ruth Gregory Collection)

By next spring, the rush was on. The town was surveyed, streets laid out and most of the timber in the Ouray area cut down for cabins. On October 2, 1876, the town was incorporated. However, most of the northern part of the county was still part of the Ute Indian Reservation. By winter the town had over 400 inhabitants, 214 cabins and tents, a school, four stores, two blacksmiths, two hotels, a saw mill, an ore sampling works, a post office, and the usual number of saloons and gambling houses that followed a new town.

Ouray County was established from the northern part of San Juan County on January 18, 1877. The first county commissioners' meeting was held March 7, 1877. The town of Ouray was designated the county seat and at the November general election the appointment was made permanent. Jess Benton, later Sheriff, soon built the new two-story county courthouse (called Benton Hall) which was the first frame building in Ouray. At first it was used as a combination courthouse, city hall and church. Later, it was to be used as a saloon, schoolhouse, armory, livery stable and blacksmith shop.

Ouray County and the City of Ouray were named after Chief Ouray. Although in the writings of some of the "latter-day" historians it is often stated that "Ouray" means "arrow," it is likely that he was never called by that name. Rockwell reports that "Chief Ouray once told Major James B. Thompson, agent for the Denver Utes, that there was no meaning to his name." "He said that 'Ooay' was the first word he spoke as a child; so his parents called him that." White people made it out to be "Ouray" but the Indians had difficulty pronouncing "r," so to them it became "Oolay."

Chief Ouray and his attractive, talented wife, Chipeta. We assume that this photo was made on one of several trips to Washington, where they were always treated as visiting heads-of-state. Both were dignified and gracious—not savages as many suppose. (Colorado Historical Society)

Chief Ouray, as were most of the Utes, was short (about 5 feet 7 inches) and stocky. He was the son of an Apache mother and a Tabeguache Ute father. When he was 18, he traveled to Colorado and soon became famous among the Utes as a ferocious fighter. His first wife, Black Mare, died only a few years after their marriage. He later married Chipeta, who originally was a slave girl who watched the child of his first marriage, but she eventually became as well known and famous as Ouray.

Chief Ouray had acted as an interpreter at the Conejos Peace Treaty meeting in 1863 when the Utes entered into the treaty that had given up most of present-day Colorado east of present-day Gunnison. He translated Ute into Spanish which was in turn translated into English. Although in early life he spoke only limited English, Chief Ouray spoke fluent Spanish as he was raised near present-day Taos and went to missionary school.

At this meeting, it was actually the white man that decided that Ouray should be chief of all the Utes. Until that time they had no overall chief, but rather many chiefs that acted by majority vote. Ouray managed through forceful personality to gain general control over the Utes.

It is generally agreed that Ouray gave up the San Juans and entered into the 1873 Brunot Treaty for two reasons. First, the white man had taken over much of the land that was ceded anyway. It was said that Ouray hoped to pull the borders back and make a new start at keeping the white man out of the new territory. Another very important reason was that Brunot managed to get a promise from Ouray that he would cooperate in the treaty negotiations if Brunot could find his son by Black Mare. The Arapahoes had stolen the child at age four, and raised him as one of their own. Since Ouray had no children by Chipeta it was a heartbreak that he carried. After Ouray persuaded the Utes to ratify the treaty, Brunot did manage through the Bureau of Indian Affairs to find the son. But when the two were reunited, Ouray's son refused to acknowledge that he could be the offspring of the chief of the enemy tribe. As part of the treaty, Ouray was also given a furnished house, livestock and 400 acres of land on which is located the present-day Ute Museum on the outskirts of Montrose.

A 1905 pamphlet summed up the contemporary white man's feelings toward Ouray when it reported that:

"... prior to 1881 the Ute Indians held undisputed possession of the Uncompahgre Valley. The head of all their tribes was Chief Ouray, who for many years swayed a scepter of such equity that he was known as the 'white man's friend.' Never in all his dealings with the whites did he show himself other than their friend, tried and true. Once, while in council with the whites upon some important matter, one of the under chiefs arose and began a tirade against the white man; old Chief Ouray listened for a moment, and with the fire flashing from his eyes he arose leveling a six shooter at the turbulent speaker, uttered one word, 'hikee,' which is Ute for 'get out.' The under chief well understood the meaning of the command and scrambled for cover, when the meeting was continued to its conclusion without further interruption. Chief Ouray died in 1879 (sic) and now the old settlers of the valley speak of him, with a strange mist in their eyes, as being a noble man with a great heart.''

Chief Ouray died at Ignacio on August 24, 1880. Chipeta lived another 44 years and died on August 16, 1924 at Bitter Creek, Utah.

Chipeta after she had grown old. The lines in this wonderful old face reflect the many years of hardships and sorrows, yet the light in her eyes and the set of her lips indicate a still stoic, brave spirit. (Ruth Gregory Collection)

Chipeta in the doorway of her "home." Information accompanying this picture indicates that it was taken in the "Garden of the Gods" in 1911. That would be 31 years after the death of Chief Ouray. (Denver Public Library)

The population of Ouray County in 1880 was reported to be 2,669 (about the same as its present population) and the assessed valuation of property was at $220,662. On February 19, 1881, Dolores County was carved out of Ouray County and Rico was made the county seat of the new county. In September of the same year, the Utes were forced out of the northern part of the county. On February 27, 1883, Ouray County was made even smaller when what is now San Miguel County was created by act of the state legislature. Telluride was made the new county seat. For a short time, some confusion reigned since the new county was called Ouray while the name of the original Ouray County was changed to Uncompahgre. However, four days later on March 3, 1883, the original Ouray County got its name back and the new county's name was changed to San Miguel. The present county boundaries are the same as in 1883 with the southern line taking a precipitous course along the ridges of the high mountains between Lake City, Silverton and Telluride. Ouray is one of the smallest (and highest) counties in Colorado with 542 square miles.

For a region that would someday be known for its rich mines, the San Juans started very slowly. There was no ore shipped in 1874; $90,517 in 1875; $244,663 in 1876, $377,472 in 1877 and $434,089 in 1878. Actually, much more ore was mined than was shipped, but since a burro only carried 1/10 ton and a mule 1/7th, the high transportation costs made it unprofitable to freight anything but the richest ore. The rest was stored in dumps outside of the mines, where some of it sits even today. The principal deposits of minerals in the Sneffels District were discovered between 1875 and 1881, except for the area's most famous mine. The Camp Bird's gold was not recognized by early-day miners who passed over the unfamiliar ore as worthless while prospecting the Imogene Basin.

"Red Mountain and mining works in vicinity." The area pictured is usually referred to as the Guston Camp. (Colorado Historical Society)

Rio Grande Southern passenger train atop 10,222-foot Lizard Head Pass. Though not so very high, as Colorado mountain passes go, this region is given to strong winds during winter storms which create monstrous drifts. A train, stalled between drifts here would have to be abandoned with the engine's boiler drained until the tracks could be opened and the engine towed into Ophir or Rico. (Denver Public Library)

Next to be discovered were the silver mines to the south in the Red Mountain District which began full production in 1882. The Red Mountain mines shipped their ore via Silverton on the Silverton Railroad which was completed in 1888 as the first of Otto Mears' narrow gauge lines. However, production abruptly halted in 1893 when the federal government stopped supporting the price of silver. The shipping of ore and concentrates from the Ouray area to smelters was a problem until the Denver and Rio Grande Railroad was built from Montrose to Ouray in 1887. With rail access to smelters, most mines of the Uncompahgre District (which surrounds the City of Ouray) were soon in full production again, as low-grade ores could now be profitably mined.

In the fall of 1882, rich strikes were made on Red Mountain and a wagon toll road was built the following year, in part by Otto Mears. This "cliff-hanger" gave direct access to the area and would eventually become "The Million Dollar Highway."

Conditions were good in the San Juans and with the Utes gone, mining could proceed at its own pace. By the end of the nineteenth century, the Camp Bird Mine alone was producing as much $3 million in one year. Wages were only $3.50 to $4.00 for ten hours' work, but they were generally the highest wages that were paid in the State of Colorado at the time. The coming of the Rio Grande Southern in 1891 and the Silverton Railroad to Red Mountain in 1888 (both owned in large part by Otto Mears) spurred a whole new interest in mining since freight costs dropped almost overnight from $25 or $30 per ton to $8 to $9 per ton when shipped on the railroad.

In 1890, the Rio Grande Southern Railroad was being built from the site of present-day Ridgway to Durango via Lizard Head Pass and the

29

town of Ridgway was surveyed and platted. Ridgway was to serve for over sixty years as the headquarters and shop area for the railroad. A large roundhouse, turntable, store rooms, shops and a depot (now moved and used as a private residence) were built. Unfortunately, fires later ravaged much of the area. Several motion pictures have been filmed at or near Ridgway including "How the West Was Won," "Tribute to a Bad Man," and "True Grit." Some of the Ridgway buildings still display the signs installed and remodeling done when the last named movie was filmed.

Although Ouray County was hurt by the demonitization of silver, conditions were not as bad as in many parts of Colorado as there was a considerable amount of new gold production occurring within the area. Rich discoveries were made in the Gold Hill area (also known as Lookout Mountain) to the northeast of town. In 1896, Tom Walsh discovered the fabulously rich Camp Bird Mine from which he was to take millions and sell for millions more. By this time, all of the major mining areas of the county had been developed. The Red Mountain area operated in the extreme southern portion of the county, the Sneffels district operated in the extreme western portion and the Uncompahgre and Paquin districts operated near the center of the county just north of the town of Ouray.

Ouray was not a "typical" rough mining town. The founders were, for the most part, well educated, professional men and managed to maintain control of the town's government and growth; therefore, Ouray was never the "rip-roaring" boom-town that writers of the "Old West" so love to tell about. Ouray had a good number of females almost from its inception. In 1880, there was a population of 402 females as compared to 2,267 males. By 1900, the ratio had increased even more to 1,714 females and 3,017 males. There was also always a relatively high percentage of children in the county as "family men" arrived early.

After 1900, Ouray County entered into a cycle of boom or bust. The population generally decreased at the rate of about one hundred persons a year until the 1940s when the demand for metals during World War II finally stabilized the population.

In more recent times the chief producer in the area was the Idarado, which was a consolidation of many famous mines mostly located on the Telluride side of the Red Mountain area. The interconnected workings total over 90 miles! The ore was taken out at the portal near the Pandora Mill east of Telluride.

In the past hundred years, prospecting methods have advanced from the hit-or-miss efforts of the early miner with his burro to the use of satellite photos, remote-sensing electronic equipment, geophysics, seismological measurement of formations' resistance to shock waves and deep diamond drill explorations.

But the history of the area is not solely the history of mining. Following the prospector were the storekeeper and the rancher. They built the towns to supply the mines and worked the farms and ranches to feed the thousands who flocked into the area. And with the arrival of the railroads, early tourism came to Ouray. Drawing cards were the scenery, the hot springs and the gothic-styled Beaumont Hotel which opened its doors in 1887, a scant five months before the railroad came to Ouray. The hot springs pool was built in the City of Ouray in 1926. Box Canyon Park was later purchased by the city. Noted writers of the day extolled the scenery of the San Juans, wrote poetry to describe its beauty and crowned Ouray the "Gem of the Rockies."

But it was the early miners' trails and wagon roads, which were often blasted and dug from solid rock to get to their upland diggings, that made this rugged country so easy to view. After World War II, with the advent of the Jeep, these rough roads evolved into a network of four-wheel-drive routes which now provide the southwestern Colorado tourist with an outstanding opportunity to reach the old workings, the ghost towns and the scenic vistas off the beaten track. There are now thousands of abandoned shafts, tunnels and cuts within a ten-mile radius of Ouray. Numerous old ghost towns slowly crumble into dust, but the scenery remains awesome.

It is truly one of the most inspiring areas of the world.

Some of the old mines, such as this one, were entered by means of a "shaft" which is a vertical hole. Miners were lowered down in "buckets" or "cages" and the ore was hoisted out in the same manner. Great care should be used when examining such sites and small children should never be allowed to run free. Most of these old properties are still owned by someone and vandalizing or removing souvenirs from the sites can be treated as any other theft. (Bill Fries III)

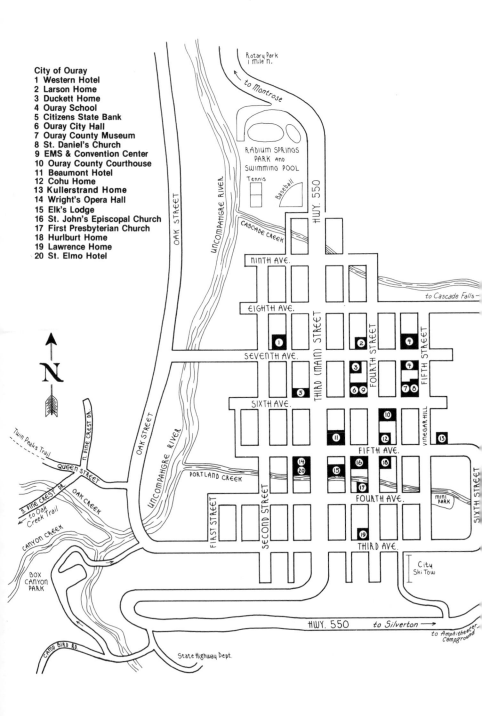

City of Ouray
1 Western Hotel
2 Larson Home
3 Duckett Home
4 Ouray School
5 Citizens State Bank
6 Ouray City Hall
7 Ouray County Museum
8 St. Daniel's Church
9 EMS & Convention Center
10 Ouray County Courthouse
11 Beaumont Hotel
12 Cohu Home
13 Kullerstrand Home
14 Wright's Opera Hall
15 Elk's Lodge
16 St. John's Episcopal Church
17 First Presbyterian Church
18 Hurlburt Home
19 Lawrence Home
20 St. Elmo Hotel

CHAPTER 3
City of Ouray
The Gem of the Rockies

The names "Gem of the Rockies" and "Opal of the Mountains" were applied to Ouray early in its existence. In addition to the lure of precious metals it was the area's scenery which attracted Ouray's earliest tourists, artists and writers.

If Ouray is the gem, it has a setting to match. Three waterfalls are either in the city limits or a short distance away. Five creeks flow into the Uncompahgre River within the town's boundaries. The Amphitheatre, east of the city, is a huge glacial cirque carved out during an ice age of almost a million years ago. If you look carefully at the middle edge of the Amphitheatre, you should be able to make out Cleopatra reclining on her couch. At an elevation of 8,400 feet in the lower area of the bowl is a 30-site U.S. Forest Service fee campground with full accommodations in the summer (May 31 to September 30). It can be reached from U.S. Highway 550 by a paved access road to the south of the city. Various hiking trails within the Amphitheatre may also be reached from the campground. A good trail map is located at the end of the paved road. The trail to the Chief Ouray Mine offers a steep two-hour to three-hour hike, but spectacular views. Follow about a dozen switchbacks and then sweep around to the north. The mine is at an elevation of 10,000 feet and several old buildings still remain. Hiking in the southeast corner of the Amphitheatre is limited as there are several private mines including the Portland Mine and a 6,000-foot tunnel that was started under the Amphitheatre toward the Grizzly Bear Mine on Bear Creek. However, Portland Trail provides a gentle four-hour or five-hour walk through the area. The Amphitheatre also provides excellent cross country skiing in the winter.

The town of Ouray is surrounded by colorful cliffs of maroon, purple, grey and yellow. To the east, Cascade Creek seems to jet out from a narrow slot in the wall of the Amphitheatre and plummet hundreds of feet downward. A short fifteen-minute hike is available to the falls beginning at the east end of Eighth Avenue. Colorful vegetation, varying in colors with the change of seasons, covers the mountains surrounding Ouray. In the winter, deer and Rocky Mountain Big Horn sheep scramble about the cliffs and even descend into the ballpark next to the pool in search of food. Herds of elk frequently come near the town.

On the southwest side of Ouray is an unusual geologic feature—Box Canyon Falls. The waters of Canyon Creek across the ages have worn a narrow gorge through which the waters descend in an unending roar that shakes the earth. At one time the falls were the intake for the town's

A reasonably current picture of Ouray, looking to the north from a position on the Million Dollar Highway. The town of Ouray is now a National Historic District, meaning at least 80% of its structures would qualify for the National Historic Register. (Bill Fries III)

hydroelectric plant. Before, tourists would walk up the bank of the creek and look at the falls, but they could not enter. Now, a walkway alongside the pipe makes the interior of Box Canyon accessible to the general public. The City of Ouray now permits visitors (for a small charge) to walk back along a path and catwalks to the very base of the falls. Here, waters descend through corkscrew-shaped chambers in the solid rock more than 200 feet vertically and then out through a narrow channel to flow into the Uncompahgre River. By taking a short but steep hike, one can reach the high bridge directly over the falls. Small evergreen trees grow out of cracks in the gorge in several places, nourished only by the spray from the falls. In the summer, Box Canyon Park is a favorite picnic area. In winter, the chamber becomes a fairyland of ice.

Not far from Box Canyon are several natural hot mineral springs. Water from them is piped to the north end of town to heat the large municipal swimming pool to a temperature near 102 degrees. There are several other geothermal springs in the city, some of which are used to heat local motels and spas. In the early years, the Utes came to Ouray to bathe in these springs.

To the west of the city are the Twin Peaks which can be reached by a trail which begins at the old city reservoir about 1/8 of a mile up Queen Street from Oak Street. Follow the signs from the intersection of Pinecrest Drive and Queen Street. The trail is very steep, three miles long and reaches 10,800 feet at the top of the easternmost peak. At 9,250 feet, the trail reaches a flat bench and forks. The right fork descends to the river road north of Ouray near the Silver Shield Mill. The upper half of the trail ascends through a thick spruce and aspen forest until it reaches the ridge immediately below Twin Peaks. By traveling on up Pinecrest Drive, left from Queen Street, one can also hike the Oak Creek Trail which traverses the same mountain. Abandoned mines on Twin Peaks include the Grand View, which was worked extensively in the 1880s and 1890s for gold and iron pyrites, and the Stenographer and Cabinet Maker mines discovered by James T. Pierson (a cabinet maker who made caskets and thereby became Ouray's first undertaker) and W.R. Alexander (a stenographer). The Oak Creek Trail requires three to five hours for the ascent only. However, the view of Ouray and surrounding peaks is unsurpassed from any other vantage point.

A walking tour of Ouray provides a view of the designs of some of the unusual storefronts on Main Street which include elaborate sheet metal, decorative brickwork and detailed bracket and cornices enhancing the Victorian flavor of the town. The private homes listed and some of the "public" buildings are not open to the public, but should be viewed from the sidewalk with respect for the owners' privacy.

The tour begins at the Ouray County Historical Museum on Sixth Avenue near the corner of Fifth Street. The building is constructed of native stone and brick manufactured locally, and originally opened as St. Joseph's Hospital in 1887 under supervision of the Sisters of Mercy. The building is Italianate in style with bracketed roof overhang and a Greek revival entrance.

A Jackson photo, copyrighted in 1901. Mountains at left contain uplifted layers of sandstone, deposited over many eons of time. At right is the amphitheatre, composed of striated layers of volcanic ash, the result, we are told, of a great eruption occurring in the Gunnison area, some millions of years ago. The hump-like hill in the foreground just beyond the city is the ancient moraine deposited there by the glacier that carved the big cirque that is the ampitheatre. (Colorado Historical Society)

35

A very old interior picture of Box Canyon. To the left of the man on the catwalk may be seen the big pipe that carried water from the top of the falls to the "Pelton Wheel" that powered one of Ouray's first electric light plants. (Colorado Historial Society)

St. Joseph's Hospital in the teens. One of the nuns of the order Sisters of Mercy, who owned and operated the hospital, may be seen standing at the entrance. (Note the cross on the roof over the portico.) The hospital, closed and replaced by a modern clinic in 1958, is now the Ouray County Historical Museum. (Ruth Gregory Collection)

The Sisters operated the hospital from the time of its beginning until continued economic problems compelled them to sell it to Dr. C.V. Bates in the latter part of 1920. Dr. Bates operated the facility as "Bates Hospital" until he retired in 1949. Two of the larger mining companies in the country acquired the hospital from Dr. Bates, and kept on a staff of nurses and retained Dr. Spangler as its principal physician. In the 1950s, the State of Colorado demanded that the hospital be brought up to modern standards (one thing they required was the installation of elevators). In 1958, the mining companies chose, rather than spend the money on remodeling the old building, to build a smaller clinic at Third Avenue and Second Street. St. Daniels Church, located next door and fearful that the old building might be sold and put to some detrimental use, prevailed upon the Pueblo Diocese to purchase the building as a protective measure. In 1971, when the newly-organized Ouray County Historical Society needed a home for the development of the museum, it was able to rent the old hospital for a token sum. Later on, the Pueblo Diocese expressed willingness to sell the building to the Society, again for a nominal amount.

Although the Pueblo Diocese and St. Daniel's Church no longer have any physical ties to the old hospital building, Father Danowski and Father Doll have, as "next door neighbors," given generously of their individual time and efforts in aiding the development of the museum and in keeping up the museum grounds.

The museum offers an excellent view of the area's past. Photographic displays throughout the building recall all the facets of local early history with surrounding mines and mining camps shown in their heyday. A mineral display and exhibits of mining machinery are designed to familiarize the uninitiated with the workings of this industry. Other displays deal with early mercantile establishments, ranching, transportation (including narrow gauge railroads), the Walsh family whose Camp Bird Mine is the most famous in the district, an operating room, an early dentist's office, an early hospital room and much more.

At 510 Fifth Avenue is the Reynolds home, built in 1895 of Queen Anne architecture with numerous spindles, curlicues and stained glass windows. A tower and lightning rod are typical of the period. The home was built by George Kullerstrand, a Ouray contractor to whom credit belongs for several of Ouray's fine houses. He was quite skilled in the production of items for "gingerbread" ornamentation. Kullerstrand and a partner by the name of Reynolds were the contractors who built the lower portion of the City Hall in 1900. The second story, paid for by Thomas Walsh, was built by a contractor, J.L. Murphy, who apparently underbid Kullerstrand and Reynolds.

On Fourth Street at Fifth Avenue is the Cohu house, built in 1888 by Dr. W.W. Ashley. The house was occupied by a series of doctors, judges and mine executives. It is an outstanding example of Queen Anne architecture and was completely restored in 1973.

On Fourth Street across Fifth Avenue is the Hurlburt house, originally owned by the Gillespie family who were in-laws to the Hurlburts. It was built in the mid-1880s and rebuilt in 1894 by George R. Hurlburt, a surveyor and engineer who was one of the locators of the Bachelor Mine. Both exterior and interior designs and period furnishings fit this Queen Anne home into the Ouray setting.

On Fifth Avenue near Fourth Street is the oldest church building still standing in Ouray, St. John's Episcopal Church. It reflects the stonework of Cornish stone masons. The Cornish as well as the Welsh and English were among the first who came to work in the mines. Carved woodwork in the sanctuary is typical of many small churches in rural England. What was to originally have been the church basement was built of stone, but finally roofed over as it was in February 1880. Matching the early stonework of the church is the connecting vicarage/parish hall building which was built in 1977 by members of the church.

At the corner of Fourth Avenue and Fourth Street is the First Presbyterian Church. The Presbyterian faith was the first to build a church in Ouray, which was only the second church built on the Western Slope of Colorado. Rev. Sheldon Jackson and Rev. George M. Darley from Lake City established the church in the summer of 1877 and Rev. Darley, a carpenter, personally directed construction upon what is now the site of the St. Daniel's Catholic Church. The original building was lost at a foreclosure sale in 1884 and the present church was built in 1890. Although fire seriously damaged the interior in 1943, it was restored and many of the furnishings saved. The eastern annex was added in 1948. The bell came from the 1883 Ouray schoolhouse which was torn down in 1938.

At Fourth Street and Third Avenue is the Lawrence home built in 1896 by G.E. Kullerstrand for a family named Tanner. Only five families have owned this house with its Dutch mansard roof. To the west is located the

Home of B.P.O.E. No. 492 built in 1904. This picture was obviously made just as the building was being completed. Wooden steps at the entrance have since been replaced with concrete ones. The bridge over Portland Creek on Main Street could accommodate only one vehicle at a time. (Denver Public Library)

carriage house which, in earlier years, accommodated servants and horse-drawn transportation.

On Main Street, between Fourth and Fifth Avenues, is the Elks Club built in 1904, which had its formal opening on June 6, 1905. BPOE Elks Lodge No. 492 was the first on the Western Slope, organized in 1898 with Dr. W.W. Rowan as its first Exalted Ruler. The two-story brick structure is a unique combination of French Queen Anne and Romanesque architecture. The interior features an antique bar which has an interesting history. During the prohibition era, there was a private club made up of past and maybe some active members of the Ouray Fire Department and known as the "Silver Slugs." They owned and used as a clubhouse the two-story building still standing directly opposite the City Hall. They brought the old bar down from Ironton. After repeal of the Volstead Act in 1933, members began to lose interest. Finally, when there were still two or three members who could legally act on behalf of the club, arrangements were made to give the old bar to the Elk's Club and the Silver Slug building was sold to a private owner. The Elks Club also contains antique slot machines (not operable) and most of the original furnishings.

On the opposite side of Main Street is Wright's Hall Opera House, built in 1888 with cast iron piers supporting the Meskar Brothers pressed metal front (perhaps the only such front of its kind remaining in Colorado). The original owners, George and Ed Wright, also owned the Wheel of Fortune Mine. The second story has a large stage and a dance floor with a seating capacity of almost 500. The lower floor has been used as a hardware store and garage. The local post office was housed in the building for a short while.

The building at the right, known simply as "The Wright Building," was built in 1881 and, at the time, said to be the largest building in Ouray. The upper story contained 21 rooms, 12' x 14' with 10' ceilings. The bottom levels were used, at different times for many purposes—a saloon, church services, skating rink, productions of the "Thespian Society," etc. The large building, "Wright's Hall," but commonly called "Wright's Opera House," was built in 1888. The top floor was used for both local and traveling theatrical productions, dances, town meetings and even for high school basketball games before 1937. For many years, the street level was a hardware store and still later, a service garage. (Bill Fries III)

The fabulous and beautiful Beaumont Hotel, built in 1886 and about which many a ridiculous myth and hoax has been invented and often written in recent years; more's the pity! In the street, the Circle Route Stage, with its team of powerful, fleet "sixes," about to begin its run to Ironton and Red Mountain. (Denver Public Library)

The St. Elmo Hotel, which is located next door, was built in 1899 by Kittie Heit. She ran a restaurant in what is now the patio area to the north.

On Main Street at the corner of Fifth Avenue is perhaps the outstanding building in Ouray, both in appearance and in its history, the Beaumont Hotel. It is on the National Historic Register. The building of the Beaumont was not so simple as some chroniclers indicate. Financing was a problem throughout the building period and "cost overruns" were a fact of life, then as now. A letter from Hubbard Reed, one of the incorporators, to F.G. Patterson to see if he could place some stock states "the building cost us a little more than we had figured on and we need $10,000 to pay off what is due the bank here and to pay up the balance that is due the contractors." Another paragraph in the same letter dated June 8, 1887 states "the building is a three-story stone and brick with a slate roof and cost $85,000." Then, as now, there were delays. The opening at one time was set for a date in April 1887, but did not come about until the end of July 1887.

From the same letter quoted from above, there is the following:

"On the ground floor is the bank on the corner, occupied by the Miners and Merchants Bank; next to that is a room rented to a mining exchange and used also as the office of P.S. and R. Company and next to that is a large room rented to a dry goods firm. Back of the bank is a barber shop.

41

"The rest of the building makes the hotel proper. In it are forty-six sleeping rooms. The building was rented cheap to secure tenants without delay. The bank pays $100 per month, the small store $75 and the large one $85. The barber shop, $50 per month.

"The hotel proper was rented till January 1st for $100 per month. After that we expect $250 or $300. (Ed. note: The hotel proper was rented to Col. C.H. Nix, proprietor of the Albany Hotel in Denver)."

As is so often the case with history, the story of the Beaumont has become a mixture of fact and fantasy. It is very probable that Herbert Hoover, at some time, stayed at the Beaumont. It wouldn't have created any stir at the time, for Mr. Hoover was then a mining engineer in the employ of large mining syndicates. He was sent by them all over the world to investigate mining properties in which his employers were interested. At that time, he had not yet become a public figure. As to Teddy Roosevelt, Sarah Bernhardt and King Leopold, surely a visit to Ouray by any of these could not have been kept secret until the late 1950s when the first written accounts appeared. As to the stories that "Thomas Edison" (sometimes it's George Westinghouse) personally installed the wiring in the Beaumont; they seem too ridiculous for anyone to believe, yet they continue to be repeated in stories written about the Beaumont.

The Beaumont's furnishings and decorations were lavish. The walls were adorned with fine redwood and pine paneling, gold velour wallpaper and an art collector's dream of fine paintings. A huge two-story ballroom and dining room were on the second floor. Only the finest furnishings were used throughout. In the lobby were several large enlargements of Wm. H. Jackson photos (about 36x40 inches) in beautiful antique frames. Unfortunately, the Beaumont's imposing exterior has deteriorated badly since 1966 when it was closed to the public.

The present Citizens State Bank building was originally the Manion Beavers Corner Saloon with a restaurant in the back. The elevated concrete sidewalk was built to allow lady restaurant patrons to bypass the saloon. The bank was originally organized in 1913 and was located in the Beaumont. However it bought the saloon during prohibition and moved in 1918. The upstairs has been used as professional offices.

On Seventh Avenue near Second Street is the Western Hotel, the largest wooden structure in Ouray. Built in 1892, it billed itself as the "miner's palace, 43 sleeping rooms, three toilets, one bathtub, electric lights, saloon and game rooms." The Western Hotel was also at the end of the red light district which ran down Second Street. The Clipper, Bon Ton, Bird Cage, Monte Carlo, Temple of Music, Morning Star and Gold Belt offered liquor, gambling, sex, dancing and music. About 100 girls operated out of the area.

On Seventh Avenue at Fourth Street is the Larson home, built in 1895 by Judge William Story. At one time after a quarrel with the power company, Story installed an electric power generator in his basement, powered by the water from city mains, which were not and still are not metered. He later returned to commercial power due to the noise made by the machinery. The house later served as a boardinghouse and from 1934 to 1975, as a mortuary run by Mr. and Mrs. Leo (Tuffy) Flor. The Queen Anne-styled structure has dormers, bay windows, gabled roofline,

The three-story, all frame Western Hotel, built in 1891. This hotel offered good sleeping rooms and fine dining, both at more conservative rates than some of the competition. It became famous, particularly during the years that "Ma" Flor owned and operated the hotel. (Bill Fries III)

porches, and leaded glass windows characteristic of the era.

On Seventh Avenue across the street is the Duckett house built by Louis King in the mid-1880s. King was a carriage maker and built this house as well as the Story Block business structure on Main Street at Seventh Avenue. After financial troubles, he sold the business building to Judge William Story who gave it his own name. The house has parquet wooden floors and Dutch tile fireplaces.

The Ouray school is to the east of the Duckett house. Ouray's first school was established in 1876 and forty-three children were in attendance by 1877. In 1883, a large building was built where the playground is now located. The present building was built in 1937-38 (and the old one razed in 1939). The present school was extensively remodeled ᵗ 1977.

At Fourth Street and Sixth Avenue is the Ouray County Courthouse built in 1888. The building is built of local bricks and with Romanesque characteristics typified by the mansard-capped cupola. A large, old-fashioned courtroom occupies most of the second floor. This was used as a setting for the courtroom scene in the movie, "True Grit," which starred the late John Wayne. Most of the original furnishings are still in the building while hallways leading to first-floor offices are now lined with prize-winning paintings of the Ouray County Arts Association. A smaller brick building to the rear houses the county offices and a jail which is no longer in use.

The contractor who built the courthouse was Francis P. Carney, one of the early residents of Ouray and destined one day to hold the second highest office in the state. Carney not only was the builder of the County

Ouray County Courthouse, built in 1888 and still in use. We're rather nostalgic about our old courthouse; we really don't want a new, up-to-date one. Neither do we want to trade the old fixtures and furniture for new, modern metal equipment. (A few years ago, the state took it for granted that we would be happy to have some nice, new metal fixtures in exchange for our "old stuff.") Ouray County taxpayers paid for the courthouse and the fixtures in it; it's ours and we want to keep it! (Bill Fries III)

Courthouse but he also supplied the brick from which it was made, for he was owner and operator of the brickyard located on the Blake Placer where the municipal swimming pool and the fish pond are now located. That site supplied most of the materials for building Ouray's earliest brick structures—the Beaumont, Wrights Hall, the City Hall, the Story Block, Manion and Beaver's Saloon (now Citizen's State Bank). Prior to the coming of the railroad near the end of 1887, it would have been impossible to freight in brick by wagon and still keep pace with the construction of many of those buildings. Even after the railroad came, the cost was almost prohibitive. The Hess Block has a facade of "imported" brick but the rest of the brick is of local manufacture.

In 1879, Carney was elected to the Board of County Commissioners for a term of three years but resigned after serving one year, for he found that time spent on county business was hurting his own enterprise and, after all, those were "boom" years in the building of permanent structures in Ouray. But the die was cast for a political career. In 1892, he was elected to the Colorado House of Representatives for a term of two years, where he was a leading member of the 9th general assembly. In 1894, he was elected to the state senate where he served four years "with much honor to himself and constituents." He was elected Lieutenant Governor in 1898. His long experience in Colorado legislative matters made him "one of the best presiding officers the Colorado Senate ever had." And he also acted as the state's chief executive. Governor Thomas did considerable traveling and was absent from the State Capitol a great deal, leaving Carney to perform the duties of governor for much of his term.

On Sixth Avenue between Main and Fourth Streets is the Ouray City Hall. It was built in 1900 and was originally a handsome building with a

A goodly portion of Ouray's population turned out to witness the ceremony of the ground breaking for the Ouray County Courthouse in 1888. (Ruth Gregory Collection)

In the "Reading Room" of the Walsh Library, Mildred McGee is sitting at the end of the table in conference with a patron. It has been estimated that the disastrous fire of January 1950 destroyed books having a value of $300,000, perhaps worth more than the building itself. (Ruth Gregory Collection)

facade and bell tower resembling a miniature Independence Hall. At first, the second floor contained an elaborate library and natural history collection donated by Thomas F. Walsh of the Camp Bird Mine. The donation included 6,589 volumes, furnishings of beautifully carved wood, a mineral collection and stuffed animals and birds. He also paid for construction of the second story. In January 1950, a disastrous fire gutted the city hall and the library. With donations and volunteer labor, the city hall was rebuilt to a functional state. But much of the loss, especially in the library, could never be replaced. In 1988, however, the facade was restored to its original elegance. The present building in addition to city offices, contains a very fine public library. The adjoining Emergency Services Building was finished in 1983 and houses, on the first floor, the county's ambulances, mine and mountain rescue trucks and the city's fire trucks. The upper floor contains a large meeting room with kitchen facilities, smaller meeting rooms and large, modern restrooms.

There are many other buildings of unusual interest and appeal throughout the city. A particularly interesting group of residences is along Oak Street on the city's west side. A recent book by Doris Gregory details the history of each historic house on the street.

To the north of the town is Radium Springs Park and the hot springs swimming pool. The area has seen a variety of uses. Originally, Johnnie Neville's First and Last Chance Saloon and Beer Garden was located near the present-day pool. The Frances Carney Brick Yard and S.P. Gutshall's Lumber Yard were located in the area. About the turn of the century, a baseball diamond was built.

The holes created by the excavating of clay for the making of brick at Carney's brickyard seeped full of warm water that bubbled from small, hot water springs in the immediate area. Though the flow to the surface wasn't large, it was, nevertheless, sufficient to maintain a fairly constant warm temperature in the ponds. The only dilution with cooler water came from precipitation. The ancestral progenitors of the goldfish still living in the one remaining pond (since the building of the swimming pool in 1926) were transferred there from private ponds at the Wiesbaden Spa. In the early 1900s, a Mr. Weston, who had acquired that hot springs property at the east end of 6th Avenue, wished to put his springs to commercial use. The goldfish were transferred and to this day, the park's "fish pond" has been one of Ouray's more popular attractions.

But goldfish were not the only inhabitants of these environs. In 1921, Ed Washington brought a two-foot alligator back from Louisiana to live in the ponds and a fence was built to keep the animal from roaming. Washington sent for a mate and for over ten years the pair lived in the ponds with each growing to a length of over six feet.

When the swimming pool was built, it was believed that there would be sufficient hot water at the site to provide good, warm water swimming. The several fish ponds maintained a fairly constant warm temperature and, in much of the park, snow was never on the ground for more than a few hours during the cold winter months. However, the large capacity of the pool necessitated that great quantities of water from the

To the left of Louis King's wagon shop is Ouray's beautiful City Hall, built in 1900. The second story, the tower, the clock and the gold-leafed dome were the gift of Thomas F. Walsh of the Camp Bird Mine. The top floor housed the Walsh Library complete with several thousand dollars worth of books which was also part of the gift. Destroyed by fire in January 1950, the building was reconstructed to a functional state. (Ruth Gregory Collection)

city's regular water system (ice water) be used to supplement the small flow of hot water from the pool site. Otherwise, the required weekly changing of water would require not just a couple of days for the refilling, but two or three weeks! The solution was to pipe hot water from the larger springs at the river's edge just outside the mouth of Box Canyon.

The area is now nicely landscaped and is complimented by an attractive bathhouse built in 1988. The 150- by 280-foot pool provides one of the country's most unique bathing experiences.

Today, Ouray's economy is divided between a revived mining industry and summer and winter tourism. Several campgrounds and many motels are located in the city. To an increasing extent, it is becoming a home for retirees attracted to the beauty and opportunity for recreational activities, and a life whose pace they can set to suit themselves.

The big outdoor pool, built in 1926, at first supplied "cabanas" for change rooms. The flash flood on Skyrocket Creek in 1929 buried the pool in rock, gravel and mud and largely destroyed the cabanas. (Ruth Gregory Collection)

The pool was excavated and a new "bathhouse" built in 1930. Here, folks are enjoying the restored, natural hot-water pool and the new bathhouse in the 1930s. (Ruth Gregory Collection)

It was a proud day when the Ouray County Highway Department got its new dump truck with solid rubber tires (no flats to fix). Loads no longer had to be shoveled off (just on); the driver simply stepped down from the cab, fixed a crank to a shaft on a gearbox and cranked the bed up higher and higher until the cargo, whatever it was, would slide out! (Ruth Gregory Collection)

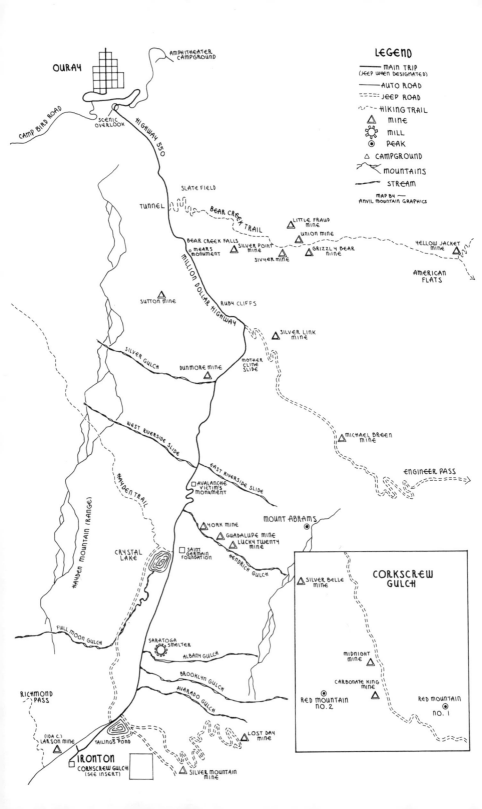

CHAPTER 4
Ouray to Ironton Park
The Million Dollar Highway

There is probably no drive in the State of Colorado offering more awesome and spectacular scenery for so many continuous miles as the Million Dollar Highway. Due to its necessarily curving design, it is not a fast road, which is an advantage, particularly to those who may be traveling it for the first time. To be carried along with fast-moving traffic when there is so much beauty and spectacular scenery would rob the traveler of his opportunity to look! Today, the road is paved and well maintained. Regardless of the impressions of some who are traveling it for the first time, there is plenty of room for everyone, so long as drivers use their own portion of the road.

Probably every other person who travels the Million Dollar Highway asks locals how it got its name. Some speculate it originally cost a million dollars to build and some say it would cost a million dollars a mile to build now. Other stories say that dumps from the mines were used that contained a million dollars in gold. Another story is that the name came from a woman who traveled the road and said "I wouldn't go back over that road for a million dollars!"

All tall tales to the contrary, the name came about in a most easily explained and as easily understood manner. In the period of 1921 to 1924 the old "Ouray and San Juan Wagon Road" was being reconstructed to make it suitable for automobile travel. By far the most difficult part was the twelve mile section from Ouray to Red Mountain Pass (the actual "Million Dollar Highway"). That twelve miles was further divided into three segments with three contracts being made with three different contractors. In a planning meeting involving the contractors, county commissioners, engineers, state highway people and the U. S. Forest Service, Lars Pilkaer (one of the contractors and the only local one) mentally summed up the bids of the three contractors. He was struck by the fact that the total was almost exactly a million dollars - a very great sum in 1922! With that on his mind, when he had an occasion to speak at a meeting, he made a remark that contained the phrase "this million dollar highway." Others at the meeting caught the significance of his remark and began using the term also. Afterwards, the phrase was innocently dropped here and there in street conversations and caught on. It was in such general use by the time of the dedication of the new highway it was simply a natural thing to make it official.

It was a beautiful road, this "Million Dollar Highway" of 1924, and the people of Ouray County were very proud of it. It was not paved, of course, and was only one-lane-wide with "turnouts" for meeting and passing oncoming traffic, but it was as up-to-date and auto-worthy as any mountain pass in Colorado in 1924. The old Model T could make it just

Some of the crowd at the ribbon-cutting, speech-making dedication of the Million Dollar Highway in July 1924. How quickly things change; only weeks ago, the stagecoach was still making its daily trips, yet not one horse-drawn rig appears in this picture. (Colorado Historical Society)

Typical scene on the Ouray to Red Mountain Road in pre-Reconstruction days. This must be a "tourister" from the flatlands; notice how tightly he hugs the cliff to the right. In the rear of the rig is a bale of hay, just in case the horses have to be fed before reaching their destination. (Colorado Historical Society)

fine if the driver kept his left foot hard down on the left one of the three pedals and the gas-lever (the one on the right, just under the steering wheel) pulled way down. Only one or two refillings of the radiator (if going up) were needed and there was water near at hand almost all the way!

It is often told, in so simple a manner, that when Otto Mears decided that the time was right, he just "up and built" the original Million Dollar Highway. Actually, it wasn't quite that easy. In the first place, as explained above, the road was never called by its present name until its reconstruction, long after Mears had anything to do with it. Mears was a builder of toll roads and well deserves the epitaph, "Pathfinder of the San Juans." Western counties, in those days, did not have revenues sufficient to provide funds for projects such as building a road up the "impossible" Uncompahgre Gorge. Men who had the know-how, the ability to organize and connections to raise finances were the answer. Toll road charters were issued whereby the builders might be reimbursed through the collection of tolls.

On April 1, 1880, the "Ouray and San Juan Wagon Road Company" filed articles of incorporation with the County Clerk of Ouray County. The stated purpose was to build a wagon road from Ouray to Mineral City with a branch running up Poughkeepsie Creek and a branch running up Red Mountain Creek into Red Mountain Park (now called Ironton Park). Capital stock was $50,000 and the life of the company was to be twenty years. At this point, Otto Mears was not yet involved.

Although progress was made in 1880, 1881 and 1882, it was nonetheless slowed by lack of sufficient finance. Stock did not find an optimistic market. In the spring of 1883, it appeared that the Ouray and San Juan Wagon Road Company was in deep trouble. There was great clamor for the branch road to Red Mountain to be finished for the region was booming, and Ouray and Silverton were competing for the business of the new camp. Apparently, in the belief that the old road company was "finished," articles of incorporation were filed on April 9, 1883 by "The Ouray and Red Mountain Toll Road Company." The stated object of this corporation was "for the purpose of building, constructing and operating a toll road between the towns of Ouray and Red Mountain." (A bit premature, perhaps.)

Two days after the above filing, the officers of the Ouray and San Juan Wagon Road Company met with the Board of Commissioners of Ouray County with a proposal to assign to Ouray County its right-of-way from the crossing of the Uncompahgre River (present Engineer Road cutoff) to Red Mountain Park, "upon the condition that the said county build a public road over the said route during the year 1883." "Viewers" were appointed to examine the route and reported favorably on April 25, 1883. On November 17, 1883, the Board of County Commissioners met in regular session and the minutes reported that: "In settlement with W.E. Block on account of building road from Uncompahgre River to Red Mountain Park"—an accounting of bills and payments, totalling $42,068.84 was reviewed and approved. Finally at this same November 17th session, "D.R. Reed, County Surveyor, presented plats of survey of line of road from Uncompahgre River to the north end of Red Mountain Park and from Red Mountain Park to Guston Gulch and upon motion, said plats were approved, ordered filed and the line of said survey declared to be a **County Road**."

That portion of the road from the Uncompahgre crossing (about three miles south of Ouray), built by the county and with public funds was, therefore, a "free" public road. The only portion of the road from Ouray to Red Mountain that was covered by the toll road charter was that three-mile stretch from town to the junction with the county road, at which point the "main-line" followed the Uncompahgre to Poughkeepsie and Mineral City.

Since the county has taken over the branch line to Red Mountain, the toll road company was able to concentrate its own efforts on the construction of the main road. Progress was being made during the early weeks of the summer of 1883, but problems of financing still plagued the builders. It was at this point that the "Pathfinder" ended their worries, for on June 14, 1883, Otto Mears concluded a deal with the Ouray and San Juan Wagon Road Company, whereby he accepted $27,000 of unissued stock (which gave him 54 percent of the total and absolute control) and agreed to complete the building of the road during that season. He put on a much larger force than had been used before and by the first week in October, eight and ten-mule outfits could work the road as far as Poughkeepsie Gulch.

All traffic between Ouray and Red Mountain, therefore, paid toll only on the three miles to the Uncompahgre crossing. To Mineral City, it was, of course, toll road all the way. With 54 percent of the stock of the toll road company, Otto Mears could call it the "Mears Road" if he wished.

Now you know the story of how, when, why and to what extent Otto Mears' name became associated with the road. When speed was needed, he had what was needed to get the job done.

To travel the present highway, begin at Ouray and follow the paved highway up the switchbacks to the south. The Camp Bird Road is the first road to the right (See Chapter 7). Then the road to the Amphitheatre Campground (open from Memorial Day to Labor Day) leads to the left (See Chapter 3). A tenth of a mile further is a spectacular scenic overlook of the town. Approximately one mile further the road passes through a tunnel built by Lars Pilkaer in 1921 as one of the major improvements to the road. Before that time the road went up a steep incline to the west of Bear Creek Hill. The dam built by Ouray Power and Light to feed the generating plant, which still operates in Ouray, is visible in the canyon. Immediately on the other side (southwest) of the tunnel is the beginning of Bear Creek Trail.

Bear Creek Trail is an extremely exciting and somewhat well-maintained hiking trail. It takes two to three hours to reach the Grizzly Bear Mine and several more hours on up the trail to American Flats and Engineer Mountain. The trail was originally on the south side of Bear Creek and was one of the principal routes on horseback or by foot from Ouray to Lake City. To take the present trail, hike from the west side of the road over the tunnel to the east. The path winds up through the pine, spruce and fir to eventually come out of the forest into a slate and shale field of the Uncompaghre Formation (this is one of the few places the formation is exposed). Hike across the slate through six or seven switchbacks. The trail then levels out at about 9,400 feet. The next mile is the "hairiest" part of the trip as there are 700-foot to 800-foot drop-offs, and slides have in some places made the trail extremely narrow. Looking across Bear Creek Canyon the Sivyer Mine's tailings are visible. The Sivyer averaged 160 ounces of silver to the ton as well as good quantities of copper and iron. The Silver Point and Painted Chief Mines were also nearby. Above the Sivyer is the Silver Queen. It was plagued with bad avalanches with one man being killed and two injured in 1899 and 1900. To the northwest are the Union,Big Fraud and Little Fraud Mines. The Union was worked only briefly, but produced both gold and silver, some assays running as high as 271 ounces of silver and two ounces of gold per ton.

Up the main trail about a quarter mile lies the Grizzly Bear Mine which was located June 16, 1875 by L. W. Balch and F. W. Sitterly. The mine reached its peak production while owned by George and Ed Wright and Milton Moore. In 1896, when George Hurlburt bought the Grizzly Bear from Wright and Moore, he switched the original trail at a cost of $8,642.09 from the shady south side of the canyon to the present trail on the north so the snow and ice wouldn't be such a problem. He dedicated the trail to the public and sold it to Ouray County in 1897 for $2,500. A small town was located at the mine with the 1900 census listing a population of 24. Unfortunately, most of the extremely rich ore (valued at over $600,000) was exhausted by that time and the inaccessability of the mine made it impossible to mine the lower grade ore.

The Grizzly Bear Mine itself is located across the creek from the few remaining buildings. A bridge used to run across the canyon from the boardinghouse to the mine.

Following the trail about two miles east you will hike steeply up the rimrock of "Hell's Half Mile," then gently travel to an elevation of 11,000 feet and the Yellow Jacket Mine. The Yellow Jacket was most active around 1915. A small mill was built and machinery hauled in before any amount of ore was discovered! From this point the trail forks. The West Trail leads to Horsethief Trail while the South Trail leads to American Flats at 12,700 feet near the top of Engineer Mountain.

Grizzly Bear Mine. There was never a wagon road or railroad to serve any of the mines up Bear Creek Canyon, only a pack trail. Therefore, the cost of bringing in supplies and shipping out ore made profits only marginal (if, indeed, there were any at all). (Ruth Gregory Collection)

American Flats is above tree line and is a smooth area of good soil and brilliant flowers and velvet grasses. Wildhorse Peak (13,271 feet), Matterhorn (13,589 feet), and Wetterhorn (14,020 feet) are easily visible.

Reversing direction, we travel the same trail to the beginning at Highway 550 and traveling south, about three-tenths of a mile from the tunnel, one comes to Bear Creek Falls. The geology of this area is extremely interesting. To the south of Bear Creek, the road cuts through the quartzite of the Uncompahgre formation. To the north are slate fields. At one time a huge glacier, probably 3,000-feet-thick, stretched from this area for 12 miles down the valley to Ridgway. The canyon was made by the glacier, not by the river (which probably has cut into the earth by no more than 50 feet). Bear Creek drops 227 feet into the Uncompahgre River. In the winter it is one beautiful blue-green icicle—a favorite for ice climbers.

The turn-out known as the ''lookout'' was built around 1921 by Lars Pilkaer. Earlier the tollgate to Otto Mears' road stood right on top of Bear Creek Falls. Toll was at first $3.75 for a vehicle with two animals, $.75 for a horse and $.35 for each pack animal. The toll keeper became kind of a living newspaper spreading news to all who passed through. A twelve-foot-wide bridge of logs crossed the top of the falls. When the toll road charter expired in 1900, the county took over the road.

Across Bear Creek Falls are the remains of the Sutton Mill. It was built by Jim and Bill Slick in 1926 and had a 100-ton capacity. The mill was mostly destroyed by fire in 1982. The mine itself is across the canyon at an altitude of 10,595 feet and was connected to the mill by a 2,700-foot aerial tramway. Other access to the mine was from the Mineral Farm area off the Camp Bird Road. The mine had four working levels with most work done in the 1920s out of the Barber Tunnel which was the one connected to the mill. The mine produced pyrite, lead, copper, silver and some gold and has been worked off and on by several groups.

Next to the road, also by Bear Creek Falls, is a monument to Otto Mears. Toll roads were not the only thing he built. In 1887, Mears began construction on the Silverton Railroad which ran from that town to Red Mountain. In 1889 he began the Silverton Northern which eventually ended in Animas Forks. In 1890 he began yet another rail line, the Rio Grande Southern Railroad, which ran from Durango to Telluride and then over the Dallas Divide to Ridgway. He had a flair for the unusual and issued silver and gold passes to his friends for use on the railroads. Mears became a powerful political figure in Colorado. He was a close friend of many Utes (he spoke their language) and he served in the state legislature. He was influential in the establishment of Lake City and Saguache and the counties of Delta, Montrose and Mesa. He helped plan the state capitol and many other state buildings. At age 77 he retired and moved to California where he died on June 25, 1931. His ashes were scattered at Bear Creek Falls. The monument was erected in 1926.

Approximately a mile above Bear Creek is the four-wheel-drive jeep road to Lake City over Engineer Pass (see Chapter 5). The Uncompahgre River passes under Highway 550 at this point. The stream that follows the highway is Red Mountain Creek. Directly to the south of Engineer cutoff the road passes beneath the Mother Cline Slide. The slide takes its name from the Mother Cline Lode, located on that same mountainside above the highway. It was one of the earliest mining claims filed in the county having been located on August 14, 1875 by Capt. Milton W. Cline,

One of several existing pictures of the tollhouse and gate at Bear Creek Falls on Mears' toll road. There was absolutely no way that the tollgate could be bypassed by wheeled rigs, although it was known to have been done by "skinners" with large pack trains, who avoided paying toll by using the Hayden Trail, from the north end of Ironton Park, over Mt. Hayden to a point on the Sneffels Road, thence to Ouray. (Colorado Historical Society)

one of the founders of Ouray and the town's first mayor. The Clines had a cabin on the hill west of Uncompahgre Creek near the main highway. Travelers and miners would often stop at the cabin for food or to warm themselves. The slide is dangerous although no one has been killed. The avalanche path itself begins only 300 feet above the highway, but covers a long distance and runs often (sometimes as much as seven times a day for four to five days in a row). In the late 1800s the slide often blocked the stage. In 1895, the Red Mountain mail carrier and his two horses swept for 100 feet down the slope. In 1906, two men were caught but uninjured by the slide. In 1975, a state snowplow received $10,000 in damage and the driver was trapped. Frequently the state shoots the slide down with howitzer cannons. Large blue icicles decorate the area in the winter.

About two-tenths of a mile past the Mother Cline, on the other side of the canyon, is Silver Gulch. The Dunmore Mine is located near the bottom of the gulch. The original mine was worked for many years and produced tungsten as well as other minerals. In the 1930s G. A. Franz bought the mine and built a tram across the canyon to the highway.

Half a mile further south is the infamous Riverside Slide. The slide takes it name from a mine (now covered) that was located right on the river. An emergency phone (often used to tell highway authorities the slide has run) is located to the north outside of the avalanche area. In earlier days the road was much closer to the creek and quite often a snow tunnel was necessary. The slide sometimes would cover the road 50 to 75 feet deep for 450 feet or more. The slide comes 3,200 feet down Riverside

Otto Mears, the "pathfinder," pictured with Chief Ouray. The two were well acquainted for both participated in several of the treaty negotiations. Mr. Mears had also acquired a conversational knowledge of the Ute language. Some writers are fond of saying that Chief Ouray liked to "affect" white man's style of dress. Although he isn't wearing the breech-clout of the near-naked savage, the clothing worn here is definitely Indian buckskin attire. Neither did he ever "affect" white man's hair style. (Ruth Gregory Collection)

The Million Dollar Highway during the late 1920s and 1930s. The rock masonry work along the outer edge of the road gave travelers an added sense of security. At that time there were no bulldozers or rotary snowplows. Snow removal was still largely a manual job to be done with shovels. The road would be closed for a few days or weeks every winter. The masonry work has since been removed to allow the big plows to dispose of the snow over the side. (Postcard view, photographed, processed and sold by Al Moule of the Busy Corner Pharmacy of Ouray - Ruth Gregory Collection)

The Riverside Slide, about four and one-half miles south of Ouray on the wagon road to Red Mountain. In former times, with no big motorized highway equipment, it was necessary to "mine" a tunnel through this mass of snow and debris deposited by this infamous avalanche. (Colorado Historical Society)

Creek from the east and Curran Creek from the west. (In 1985 a large protective snowshed was completed which has taken much of the risk out of driving the highway in the winter.) There were many reports of the Riverside running in the 1880s and 1890s with narrow escapes. The mail carrier in 1897, John "Jack" Bell, was reported killed but dug himself out after 24 hours. In December 1908, the slide took its first life, Elias Fritz, riding in a freighting sleigh coming down from Red Mountain. Several near fatalities continued in 1910 including a near miss of the stage. On March 3, 1963, the slide dealt death again, killing the Rev. Marvin Hudson and his two daughters, Amelia and Pauline.

About a quarter of a mile south above the switchbacks, a monument has been erected to honor Rev. Hudson and his daughters. They were enroute to Silverton to conduct church services when Rev. Hudson's car began slipping and he stopped to put on chains. It was a week before Rev. Hudson's body was found. Amelia's body was not found until March 17 (St. Patrick's Day) near but not in the car, which was located on the same day. Pauline was not found until May 30 of that year. The car was found downstream 600 feet from where it was swept off the road with the top torn off and the doors either open or gone. However, a jar of cream in the car was unbroken. Next to the Hudson monument is another honoring two snowplow drivers who were killed while clearing previous slides. On March 2, 1970, Bob Miller was killed while using a caterpillar tractor. On February 10, 1978 the slide struck again killing Terry Kishbaugh who was driving a rotary plow.

Traveling up the road about half a mile, the road enters a large flat area named Ironton Flats or Ironton Park. The Red Mountains are visible at the southern end. The western ridge of the valley divides the Red Mountain District from the Imogene District. The eastern ridge is known as Brown Mountain with its northern extremity being Mt. Abrams. Brown Mountain is 13,339 feet at its south end and 12,801 feet at Abrams. Geologists tell us the flats were probably formed when large mudslides from Hendrick Gulch (which enters to the east) dammed the lower end of the valley forming a lake which gradually filled with silt. Good "flatland" cross country skiing is available in this area in the winter.

The Lucky Twenty Mine (also called The York and The Guadalupe after its various tunnels that progress up the mountain) is located about half way up Hendrick Gulch. It was originally owned by T. J. York, postmaster and county clerk in Ouray in the 1890s. The mine has operated off and on to present times and has three extremely well developed tunnels at different levels. It averaged about 50 ounces of silver and 20 ounces of copper per ton of ore and veins up to 12-feet-wide were found.

The north end of Ironton Park was developed in the late 1930s as a year-round recreation area. It was a great idea but born prematurely. The late Ralph Kullerstrand and the late Joseph Condotti, in partnership, constructed the dam that formed the lake (now called "Crystal Lake"), built a ski lift with seven towers and cleared a run of approximately 1,800 feet. They razed the giant smokestack at the Saratoga Smelter and used the brick to build a fine lodge which featured kitchen and dining room lounge and sleeping rooms. Unfortunately, some disagreement arose between the two partners with the result that, though the project was completed and ready, the resort was never opened for business. The stalemate continued until members of the St. Germain Foundation ("I Am" religion) immigrated into the area in the 1940s. The property was purchased by the Foundation and occupied in the summer months. A resident watchman remained through the wintertime. One day in the winter, the watchman (also maintenance man) was attempting to melt a small patch of ice on the roof so that he could make a repair. The blowtorch he used under a "tent" constructed of a piece of canvas caught the roof on fire and the beautiful lodge building burned to the ground!

By going across the dam of Crystal Lake, one can get to the beginning of the Hayden Trail, which is approximately six miles long. In normal years this trail can be traveled safely only in July and August. It can be completed in about seven to eight hours but requires very strenuous, steep climbing. The trail doesn't appear on current topographical maps, but the forest service cleared and marked the trail in 1976 and it is in good shape. Look for the forest service blaze on the trees (!) and piles of rocks with wood. Keep going up the switchbacks to the base of some large cliffs and then basically travel on the level towards Ouray. The trail ends at the Camp Bird Road just east (toward town) near the spot where the road crosses Canyon Creek.

Traveling south through Ironton Park, several small mines are visible. The large gulch on the west is Full Moon Gulch. To the east, from north to south, are Albany Gulch, Brooklyn Gulch and Avarado Gulch, each of which once contained a mine by the same name. Albany Gulch also contains the ruins of the Saratoga Smelter and Mine. This point was the northern terminus of the Silverton Railroad. The mine was large and contained good ore; the railway station at the smelter was called Albany. By the mid 1890s, costs were too high and the area abandoned. The Saratoga was discovered in 1883 and by 1894 produced $125,000, mainly in silver with some gold. It eventually had a 1,000-foot tunnel with several levels. The Mono-Baltic, Maud S and Brooklyn Mines were in the area and all had veins of 750 to 1,000 feet.

About half a mile further south on Highway 550 is the beginning of the Idarado Mine's tailing pond to the east. The Larson Brothers (or Ida L.) Mine is visible to the right alongside the road. The mine had two veins which have been explored for about 180 to 200 feet each. The vein averaged about 5 feet wide and production consisted of silver with very small amounts of gold, zinc and lead.

A short way further up Highway 550, a small road to the west side of the highway leads up a short distance to the Beaver and Belfast Mine. The mine was an early producer and contained several thousand feet of tunnels following one-foot to four-foot wide veins of gold, silver, lead and zinc. Shortly past this mine, a trail leads up to the Greyhound Mine and on over Richmond Pass into the Camp Bird area. The trail is not maintained and passes through private property, but is a very interesting eight to ten hour hike. The mine was located to follow an extension of the Camp Bird's rich veins and has been worked off and on up to the present.

Back at the beginning of the tailings pond, a small jeep road passes over the creek just to the north of the tailings and to the right up Corkscrew Gulch. This is a spectacular shortcut from the Uncompahgre River Valley

Crystal Lake, in the north end of Ironton Park (in earlier times, known as "Red Mountain Park"). This man-made lake was built in the latter half of the 1930s, as told in this chapter. The lake and adjacent property was acquired by the St. Germain Foundation (I Am) in the mid-1940s. It was during the tenure of the foundation that the beautiful brick lodge burned to the ground. (Bill Fries III)

over the Red Mountains to Cement Creek and down to the portal of the Standard Metals Mine at Gladstone. The road was carved out of the mountains in recent years to transport diamond drilling rigs to various sites on the flanks of the Red Mountain. The road is for four-wheel-drive vehicles only and should be avoided in very wet weather because of considerable areas of yellow clay.

Traveling up Corkscrew and looking across the gulch, the famous railroad engineering site of the Corkscrew covered turntable is visible. It provided the means of turning locomotives around to get trains through a space too tight for a curve. It was the product of the inventive mind of civil engineer C. W. Gibbs who worked for Otto Mears and also designed the Chattanooga Loop and the trestles of Ophir. The turntable was used rather than backing the trains down the slope because the cars tended to derail or unhitch when the latter method was used. Gravity could be used to reverse a whole train - one car at a time. The foundation still remains, although the building that covered it has long since disappeared.

Ascending into a spruce forest, the road passes the ruins of several old miners' cabins which were built by the owners of the Midnight, Earl and Carbonate King Mines. Shortly thereafter, the road comes out into open talus slopes and begins a sharp ascent via a series of switchbacks to the 12,217-foot saddle between Red Mountain No. 1 and Red Mountain No. 2.

Descending towards Cement Creek you are afforded a view of the basins below, pock-marked with adits and dumps of mines which waxed and waned over a century of fortune hunting. After a few minutes, the road going down intersects one coming up from the former town of Gladstone. Turning to the left will take you about one mile to the remains of the ghost town of Poughkeepsie (the area is now posted). Crofutt, in his **Gripsack Guide to Colorado**, in 1885 reported that the town had "a store, restaurants, saloons, many comfortable buildings and a summer population of about 250. It is the biggest little mining camp in the San Juan country." A post office was also located at the site and L. P. Kendall was postmaster. Kendall also started the town's newspaper - **The Poughkeepsie Telegraph**. By 1890 the town was abandoned. From the vantage point of the old town site you may look down at a northeasterly direction to the deep blue water of Lake Como which was scooped out by glacial action.

Returning via the route that you ascended, you will pass the intersection and continue descending until you reach the portal and scene of operations of the gold and silver producing Sunnyside Mine. The mine includes the extensive workings of the Sunnyside Mine near Eureka and part of the Gold King Mine which was located at this spot and eventually merged with the Sunnyside. In 1899, the Silverton, Gladstone and Northerly Narrow Gauge Railroad was built to connect the townsite of Gladstone with Silverton. This provided a link with Denver via the Denver, and Rio Grande Narrow Gauge lines to Durango. The Silverton, Gladstone and Northerly is one railroad that Otto Mears did NOT build. It was promoted by the Gold King Mining Co. under President W. Z. McKinney to not only haul the ores of the Gold King but of the mines all along Cement Creek to the smelters in Silverton. It was chartered on April 6, 1899 and completed in July. The Rocky Mountain Construction Company constructed the 7.5 miles of track and the half mile of sidings between Silverton and Gladstone. In 1910, Mears, Slattery and Pitcher

The Covered Turntable in Corkscrew Gulch, on the mainline of the Silverton Railway. The gulch was so narrow that the customary "loop" could not be used, therefore, the turntable was a means of getting trains from Red Mountain Town to Ironton and return. The Silverton was claimed to be the only railroad in the world with a turntable on its mainline track. (Denver Public Library)

The Town of Gladstone. After the building of the Silverton Railway to Red Mountain and the Silverton, Gladstone and Northerly up Cement Creek to Gladstone, the road connecting Gladstone with Poughkeepsie and Red Mountain fell into disuse and was reopened only a few years ago for jeep travel. (Colorado Historical Society)

(Mears' son-in-law) leased the Gold King Mine. The same year the Silverton, Gladstone and Northerly was leased by the Silverton Northern. On June 10, 1915, the Silverton Northern bought the S.G. and N. at auction. The railroad died in 1926. Now a broad highway (first built in 1879) accommodates trucks that take ore from the mine and basically parallels old railroad grades to the Mayflower Mill, just east of Silverton, where the ore is eventually refined into concentrate and later smelted into pure gold and silver.

The town of Gladstone once housed workers of the Gold King Mine, which was discovered by Olaf Nelson in 1887 and soon began to produce extremely rich gold pyrite-quartz ore. The mine is located on the slopes above the north fork of Cement Creek at 11,400 feet. Ore was carried by a tram a mile long. Almost 200 people lived in the area of Gladstone. Several major disasters have occurred at the mine, the latest of which occurred in 1978 when miners tunneled into the bottom of Lake Emma. The resulting flood did nine million dollars in property damage, sent valuable ore for miles down Cement Creek and the Las Animas River and shut the mine down for almost two years. Luckily there were no fatalities as the flood occurred when no one was working in the tunnel.

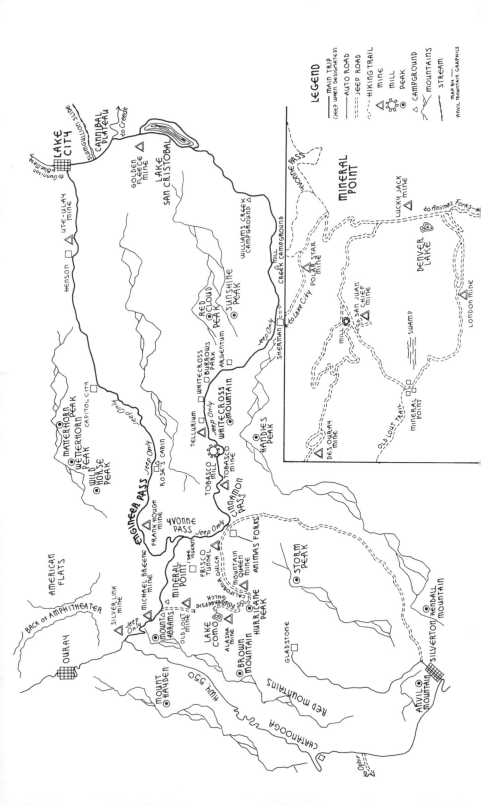

CHAPTER 5
Engineer Pass to Lake City
Path of the Prospectors

It was from Mineral Point down Uncompahgre Creek or Bear Creek that the first prospectors found their way into the high walled valley that surrounds Ouray. Some had come to Baker's Park (now Silverton) and others from Lake City. Early supply lines for freight, mail and stagecoach passage were forged from the San Luis Valley into Lake City and thence up either Henson Creek to Engineer Pass or up the Lake Fork of the Gunnison over Cinnamon Pass to supply Animas Forks and Mineral Point. The prospectors slowly worked their way down Mineral Creek and Bear Creek into the steep defiles beneath today's Million Dollar Highway. It was in 1875 that a small group of prospectors first found their way from Baker's Park to the present site of the City of Ouray, and there, near the mouth of Box Canyon, they staked claims.

The route across Engineer Pass begins at 8,850-foot elevation at the State Bridge on U. S. Highway 550. The trip to Lake City requires about four hours and the return via Cinnamon Pass takes about an equal amount of time. The road is four-wheel-drive only and is very rough in some sections. In June and July, when the snow is melting off the section of the road that crosses the flats at the base of Engineer Mountain, the roadway often contains deep mud holes. But the trip is always worth the trouble for the view from the top of the pass provides a spectacular panorama of the San Juan Range as well as a chance to view many abandoned mines.

Starting from the State Bridge the road climbs rapidly through a series of switchbacks as it follows the Uncompahgre River to the southeast. The first two miles contains some of the roughest terrain of the entire route to Lake City. After traveling about one-half mile, by looking up to the left (north), one may glimpse the dump and a few of the remaining buildings of the Silver Link Mine located at 10,500 feet. The mine was extensively developed in the early 1880s and produced an estimated $100,000.00 in silver and copper before the year 1902. Over 2,200 feet of drifts followed the vein which was sometimes up to twenty feet wide. Hand picked ore from the mine contained up to 30% copper and three hundred ounces of silver per ton.

About a mile past the Silver Link, the road passes through the workings of the Mickey Breene Mine (originally called the Michael Breene). Starting in 1890, when a mill, boardinghouse and power plant were constructed, the mine has operated off and on through the years. Silver and copper, the latter not usually associated with Colorado, are the chief metals in its veins. Hand picked ore averaged 658 ounces of silver per ton. Originally under separate ownership, but now part of the mine, is the mother lode composed of the Royal Consort, Duke of Edinburgh

At the turn off from Highway 550 onto the road to Engineer Mountain, if you bend your head way back, look northeast and UP, perhaps you may make out some remaining buildings at the Silver Link Mine. It would require a very powerful telephoto lens to get a recognizable picture from the highway. This is the only picture we have found, taken at the site of the Silver Link. (Ruth Gregory Collection)

Michael Breen Mine, located by Captain M. W. Cline in 1874 as was adjacent Mountain Monarch. The Breen has had off-and-on periods of operation—some in recent years. (Ouray County Historical Society)

and Royal Albert claims. Claim maps show the Royal Albert, the Royal Consort and the Duke of Edinburgh strung out in a line, abutting end to end and contiguous to both the Mountain Monarch and Mickey Breene. Another claim that underlaps both the Monarch and Mickey Breene, lying crosswise to each, is the Pioneer Lady. These claims were located and filed upon in September 1874 by Milton W. Cline, one of the founders and first mayor of the Town of Ouray. The filings were made almost a full year before the first prospectors reached the site of Ouray. The claims were owned at one time by a former governor of Colorado, Frederick Walker Pitkin and William Sherman and the area was sometimes called the Sherman-Pitkin Mine. The mine was worked in a big way during the 1890s, with David Reed as its chief engineer and general manager. Even in recent years, after many starts and stops, there has been some production.

About a half mile past the mine, Diamond Creek runs across the road. Shortly thereafter are several small campsites but no facilities are available.

About a mile past the Mickey Breene, the road into Poughkeepsie Gulch forks to the right and the main road to Engineer Pass curves to the left to follow Mineral Creek. The area around the fork was once laid out as the Townsite of Poughkeepsie but the actual town grew at the other end of the gulch. While the road up Poughkeepsie may be easily traversed for a short distance, it should be regarded as a dead-end.

If the Poughkeepsie Road is taken as a short side trip, at a little over a mile a large dump is visible immediately by the road. A foot trail begins at this point and ascends about 1,000 feet in elevation to the site of the Old Lout, one of the principal mines in the gulch. The Old Lout was located in 1876 and produced an estimated $400,000.00, mainly in silver, before closing in the silver panic of 1893. Several times since the mine has been reopened. The Old Lout was originally worked through a shaft at the upper workings, but in 1886, a tunnel was driven at lower levels. The Maid of the Mist is an extension of the same vein as the Old Lout. Early work produced good results in silver and lead.

Further up the road to the south of the creek is the site of the Poughkeepsie Mine. It was evidently the first mine in the area. It was located in 1873 and produced a high grade of silver-copper ore. An early offer of $30,000.00 for the mine was refused. It is located on a major vein of the entire San Juans. From here to Lake Como the road is impassable, and should be limited to hiking. Short shafts and cuts in the area of Lake Como belong mainly to the Como Group and the Alaskan Group. The Alaskan Group was at the time said to be the most prominent in the district and was purchased in 1879 by H.A.W. Tabor (Baby Doe Tabor's husband) and others for $125,000.00. Frank Fossett reported in 1880 (shortly after the purchase by Tabor) that "the mine has been steadily developed by the new owners and new buildings have been erected, including an ore house and quarters for 25 men employed." After reaching Lake Como, the road skirts to the east and passes by the Bonanza Mine. The road then climbs up a steep talus slope to the southeast near Hurricane Peak. Following the jeep trail into California Gulch, the road passes the remains of a large mine just two-tenths of a mile on the other side of the summit. This was the Mountain Queen Mine whose main shaft is 400 feet deep and connects with a 1,500-foot tunnel which comes from the lower California Gulch area. The shaft of the Mountain Queen was sunk under the direction of Thomas F. Walsh. (This is the only evidence we have found to offer any support to the story that Walsh ever lived in Animas Forks.) In a letter to his partner in Chicago, Walsh says, "The Mountain Queen pay streak does not hold its value going down. For 600 feet on the surface it averages 100 ounces. Four feet down it falls to 30." The mine has produced over $200,000.00 and was reported by Frank Fossett to have "a galena vein of great size, but of rather low average grade."

Returning to the Engineer Road and proceeding east, the Des Ouray Mine is encountered after about two miles. It received its name by virtue of investors from Des Moines, Iowa. The area is extensively developed with several mine tunnels, mining equipment, cabins and other buildings still visible. It is a collection of some twenty claims. The Wewissa, the Benach and the Eurades, all part of the many claims mined by Des Ouray, have been from time to time mined independently. The mine would then be known by the name of the claim. It has been worked on and off for years and may well open again in the near future. In 1925, a sawmill also operated out of the area. At the site of the sawmill, two steam boilers used to be seen rusting away. An inevitable question asked

Old Lout, high in Poughkeepsie Gulch. The building with the smokestack houses a boiler and engine to raise and lower the cage in the shaft. Head-frame and sheave wheel are seen between the two large buildings. (Colorado Historical Society)

by green-horns during the early years of the jeep tours was, "How in the world did anybody get those big boilers up here?" One of the jeep drivers liked to explain it this way: "Well, you see, when there was only a pack-trail, everything had to be brought up here on pack burros. Loading a pack burrow was a very particular business. Whatever was loaded on one side of the pack-saddle had to be counter-balanced on the other side so that the animal wouldn't be top heavy and maybe fall off the trail. They didn't really need two boilers but they had to bring the extra one along just to balance the load."

A mile and a quarter further, the main road curves to the left and ascends a wooded knoll which affords a good view of the deteriorating ruins of the San Juan Chief Mill. A very rough road also crosses the creek to a pack trail that eventually leads back to the Old Lout and Maid of the Mist mines in Poughkeepsie Gulch. If you stay on the main road for approximately another mile and a half, rather than crossing the creek, it is possible to enter into a tundra area and then cross back to the San Juan Chief Mill.

In the general area of this mill was the settlement of Mineral Point, which was first settled in 1873 and continued to be active until the late 1880s and early 1890s. Some latter-day historians conjecture that Mineral City is one and the same as the site of the San Juan Chief Mine and Mill. Actually, Mineral Point (Mineral City) lay at the southern edge of a swampy area a quarter mile south of the San Juan Chief. Enough traces of the street and buildings remain to establish the place upon a little examination. Also, early-day photographs and topographical maps place it at this site.

Although Mineral Point was already established and was the jumping-off point for the prospectors who came to the site of Ouray in 1875, it didn't get a post office until ONE DAY LATER than Ouray did! Ouray's post office was established on October 28, 1875, but Mineral Point didn't get one until October 29, 1875! Mineral Point's post office had one brief closure on October 14, 1878, but was reopened April 23, 1879 and continued operation until January 28, 1897. The town derived its name from the extensive mineralization and parallel veins that can be seen on the surface. The town at one time contained in addition to the post office, a store, sawmill, restaurants and saloons, and enough log cabins to shelter nearly two hundred people. The peak population of the area in the summer may have reached several hundred, but the winters were so fierce that only a few remained in the town. Ingersoll reported that "Mineral Point...is covered with claim stakes until it looks like a young vineyard." The town of Mineral Point was also known as "Apex of the Continent" even though it was not located on the Continental Divide. However, the Animas River, Uncompahgre River, Lake Fork of the Gunnison and Henson Creek all have their headwaters within a mile of the townsite. By the turn of the century, the area was completely deserted except for a few summertime prospectors. Major mines in the area included the Bonanza, the Red Cloud, the Boston and the Mastodon. Silver from 15 to 100 ounces per ton was produced.

Continuing on for about a mile from the San Juan Chief, the Engineer Road forks to the left. By traveling on to the right, the road leads first to the Cinnamon Pass cutoff to Lake City and then to Animas Forks, Eureka and Silverton areas. By taking the lefthand fork and ascending Engineer Pass, the road switchbacks up the side of 13,218-foot Engineer

Mountain. About half way up the mountain the road passes the Polar Star Mine. H. A. Woods first located this claim in March of 1875. He was in Howardsville near present-day Silverton and overheard some prospectors talking of going to the spot. That night, he took off ahead of them and arrived at the claim at 6:00 a.m. to beat them out by hours. The chilly morning at the time of his arrival gave rise to the name of the mine.

Left of center, barely distinguishable, is the San Juan Chief Mill, shut down while it was yet new because of the sudden decline in the value of silver in 1893. The town of Mineral Point was near the point where the road disappears in this picture. (Bill Fries III)

By crossing over Engineer Pass (the pass elevation is 12,800 feet), one descends to the tundra and grasslands of American Flats - an area of hundreds of acres of flat and gently rolling country located between 12,000 and 13,000 feet. The area is covered with grass and wildflowers in the summer. However, a word of warning: Since the area has no high peaks or trees, it is extremely easy for a traveler to get lost in the Flats!

Engineer City was located in the basin with the Frank Hough Mine. The Frank Hough was discovered in January 1882 and produced gray copper, copper pyrites and iron pyrites, with silver running 50 to 60

Mineral Point. Look closely, you'll find some of the town's buildings tucked away here and there among the trees. During the life of Mineral Point, all the trees, big and small, were cleanly cut off. Some of the stumps remain. Situated just at timberline, Mineral Point was one of several towns to claim, at one time or another, "the highest post office in the nation." A local justice of the peace, threatened with having one of his decisions "appealed to a higher court," retorted, "There is no higher court!" (Denver Public Library)

About all that remains of "Engineer City," this building probably belonged to the owners of the Frank Hough Mine. Bringing in wood to keep the house warm overnight and to cook breakfast in the morning was quite a chore for this house is 1,500 feet above timberline. (Bill Fries III)

Rose's Cabin at the base of Engineer Mountain on Henson Creek along the road to Lake City. Here, travelers could rest and refresh themselves for Rose's Cabin was actually an inn, with sleeping rooms, dining room and a bar. Here too, stagecoaches stopped to exchange jaded horses for fresh ones. (Ruth Gregory Collection)

ounces per ton and a trace to an ounce of gold per ton. In 1884, it produced 700 tons worth $52,500.00, but there is little evidence of any sizeable production after the turn of the century. As many as four hundred men were in the area during the summer, most boarding in tents. In the Lake City Silver World, July 1882 issue, it boasted that Engineer City was the only town of its size with no saloon.

Another two miles down the road is the site of Rose's Cabin, an early-day stagecoach stop and small settlement. The owner was Corydon Rose, a man who built a hotel and bar at that location in 1877. Until 1880, it was the only place of entertainment between Mineral Point and Lake City. The main hotel consisted of 22 tiny rooms. At its peak the population of the area was approximately 100. By 1885, Crofutt describes it as "A small mining camp on Henson Creek, 15 miles west from Lake City. The place consists of a post office, smelting works, store, restaurant and about 120 population." The post office was established June 27, 1878 and was in service until September 19, 1887.

For many years, even well into the 20th century, Rose's Cabin served as a haven for travelers, both on foot and on horseback. The Rev. George Darley who established and built the first two churches on the western slope of Colorado (the first in Lake City and the second in Ouray), had good reason to appreciate the location of Rose's Cabin on one memorable occasion. It was February in the winter of 1890 that The Rev. Darley made a trip on foot from Ouray to Lake City via Engineer Mountain in a heavy snow storm. He was accustomed to traveling long distances on foot, over, around and through the San Juan Mountains at all seasons of the year in all kinds of weather. He left Ouray at 5:00 a.m. in a blinding snow storm, traveling the trail from Ouray up the Uncompahgre River to Mineral Point, thence over Engineer Mountain, stopping once at a cabin where he obtained a warm meal and a chance to warm himself and dry his clothes a bit. At times he forced his way through snow that was waist deep and even armpit deep as he crossed over the summit of Engineer Pass. At 9:00 p.m., after sixteen hours on the trail, he gained the sanctuary of the saloon at Rose's Cabin. The miners who were lounging in the warm saloon welcomed him, congratulated him too, for to them it seemed a miracle that any human could have survived that trip over Engineer Mountain in such a storm! Darley himself swore he knew a man who took his burro over Engineer in the dead of winter by putting snowshoes on its feet!

In 1920, the barns and buildings at Rose's Cabin were remodeled and even provided modern plumbing, but in 1950 the main building was torn down. The partial remains of the hotel's fireplace and stable are still visible.

Continuing towards Lake City, the road passes through the remains of Capitol City which was a dream of George T. Lee. He built a brick mansion on the spot and envisioned himself as the governor of Colorado, ensconced in a new Colorado Capitol which was to be moved to this site from Denver. The brick mansion contained bay windows, rich paneling, a small theatre and even an outhouse modeled after the mansion. In the 1950s, Lee Mansion was still complete enough that it could have been restored and used. People could drive their Cadillacs from Lake City to this site and many a car's trunk was filled with brick, gouged out of the walls, to take home as souvenirs. By about 1960, it became necessary to bulldoze the remainder of the building from the site to eliminate the danger of people being injured by falling segments of the walls. Capitol City's post office was established May 18, 1877 and discontinued October 30, 1920. Capitol City and Lake City were the only two towns in Hinsdale County to ever be incorporated. Crofutt, in 1885, listed Capitol City's population as about 120 people. By 1896, according to Colorado Business Directory, the population was down to 50 with the nearest banking point at Lake City. It had stage service six times a week. For the next 25 years, Capitol City held its own - the population still 50 in 1920, but the nearest banking point was Montrose. At either end of the Capitol City area, the remains of the smelters owned by Lee can still be seen.

From Capitol City on into Lake City, the road is in extremely good condition having been two lanes since the time it was built as a toll road in 1877. The fishing in Henson Creek is also excellent from this point to Lake City. Five and half miles toward Lake City from Capitol City one reaches the Ute Ulay Mine and the site of Henson. The creek and town were named for a prospector who was in the area in 1871. A post office was established at Henson on May 7, 1883 but discontinued November 30, 1913. The Ocean Wave and Hidden Treasure were also nearby. During the 1880s and 1890s, between 200 and 300 men were always employed in the area. A smelter was built in 1878 and three tram cars ran up a steep incline from the mill to the mine. Although the Ute-Ulay was discovered in 1871, it was not officially located until 1874 as it was in Ute Territory until that time. It sold in 1876 for $125,000 and then again in 1880 for $1,200,000. The mine has produced exceedingly rich amounts of

Capitol City was never very much more than appears in this picture. Its founder, George Lee, had a dream of being appointed territorial governor of Colorado, and of making HIS town the capital of the state, hence the name. If he had spelled it correctly—who knows. Partial remains of the "governor's mansion," a beautiful red, brick building were there through the 1950s. For reasons of safety, it had to be "bulldozed" to the ground. (Colorado Historical Society)

Lake City, founded in 1874 as a result of Enos Hotchkiss' discovery of the mine that later became the famous "Golden Fleece." The town soon became the great hub of activity in the San Juans, preceding the founding of Silverton, Ouray and Telluride. Here, some of the most colorful, but TRUE history of the Old West was made: the trial of Alferd Packer, the "cannibal;" the trial of Ed Kelly, killer of Bob Ford who had killed Jesse James; the lynching of Betts and Browning for the killing of Sheriff Campbell. Present-day Hinsdale County claims to be the "least populated county in Colorado." (Colorado Historical Society)

galena, silver, lead and gold. Total production has probably exceeded several million dollars. It was the production records of the Ute-Ulay and the promised high-tonnage shipments that were the most persuasive arguments in getting the Denver and Rio Grande to build a branch rail line from the main-line at Sapinero to Lake City. A slump hit the mining industry shortly after the railroad arrived in 1889; then there was the panic of 1893 which all but wiped out mining in Colorado, except where there were good quantities of gold ore. Shipments of ore declined year by year after the railroad was built. Again in the 1920s, it was the promise of large shipments from the Ute-Ulay (the largest mining operation ever in Hinsdale County) that was used to block the abandonment of the railroad for several years. The great mine has been closed down for a good many years, with only spasmodic attempts to get it into operation. The mining and milling equipment had become obsolete and the owners did not have the means to bring it up to date. In 1925, Michael Burke, a wealthy mining promoter, bought the mine, brought in modern mining equipment, built a new 100-ton mill, constructed a 60-foot-high dam on Henson Creek downstream from the mine and installed a hydroelectric generating plant. It was Burke's influence that prevented the abandonment of the Lake Fork branch of the D&RG for several years; claiming that all his expenditures on the Ute-Ulay would be for naught without the means of shipping his product by rail. When the 1929 Depression came, however, metal prices were so low that Burke was never able to make the ore shipments that he had promised. In 1932, the D&RG finally had the consent of the Public Utilities Commission to abandon the line. Burke's hopes were not entirely dead, so he bought the line and tried running a railroad himself - just for the sake of his Ute-Ulay Mine. In 1937, he was obliged to give up railroading as well as operating the mine and moved to Denver. In the same year, a salvage crew began removing rails, ties and equipment from the Lake Fork line.

Four miles further downstream from Henson lies Lake City. It was originally an early distribution and transportation center as well as an operating center for the nearby mines. It lies just north of the largest natural body of water in Colorado, Lake San Cristobal, which was formed 600 to 700 years ago when the huge Slumgullion Mud Slide descended into the valley and dammed the Lake Fork of the Gunnison River. Today, the lake provides fishing and recreation which enables the community to remain a popular resort.

Lake City was built originally as a result of the discovery of the Golden Fleece Mine, but within a few years, it was the focal point for goods coming by pack train or wagon from the San Luis Valley via either Saguache or Del Norte and bound for the mines near Ouray, Silverton and Telluride. The courthouse at Lake City was the scene of the trial of Alferd Packer who was convicted of the cannibalistic slaying of five companions in 1874. After being captured he escaped, but finally was recaptured in Wyoming nine years later. He was returned to Lake City where he was convicted and sentenced to death. Later, the Colorado State Supreme Court reversed his conviction and ordered a retrial at which time he was convicted of five counts of manslaughter. Packer served 15 years of a 40-year sentence and then was paroled.

Fossett, in 1880, reported that:

> "Hinsdale County is the most easterly of the important silver districts in the San Juans. Its metropolis is Lake City dating from 1874-75 located at the junction of Henson Creek and Lake Fork of the Gunnison...There are numerous silver lodes in the lofty mountains that rise almost perpendicularly for a half mile or a mile on every side - many of them worked extensively...The site is decidedly romantic, surrounded as it is by stependous (sic) mountains...From a mere cluster of cabins in 1875 it has grown into a thriving busy center of from 1,500 to 2,000 population, its mills and reduction works comprising the most extensive system of mining machinery in all the San Juan country. It has churches of almost every denomination, three or four hotels, good schools, several banks, five saw mills, free reading room and library, two excellent and energetic newspapers and other evidence too numerous to mention of substantial and lasting prosperity."

Today Lake City is still a charming town with large cottonwoods, old Victorian homes and log cabins lining its streets. Of particular interest are the old Victorian churches of the area and the old main street one block off of what is now the main road. Hinsdale County is reported to have the smallest population of any county in the United States.

Driving south along the shore of Lake San Cristobal, one encounters the Golden Fleece Mine which was discovered in 1874 by Enos Hotchkiss, who was at the time building the Los Pinos toll road to

Silverton for Otto Mears. The mine sold in 1891 for $75,000 and produced lead, silver, gold, copper and zinc. It is producing again at present. Following the Lake Fork of the Gunnison for about four miles past the lake (both afford excellent fishing) is William Creek Campground (a fee area). Just four-tenths of a mile beyond the campground is an extremely difficult four-wheel-drive road leading off to the left of the main road and up Wager Gulch to the ghost town of Carson, which sits atop the Continental Divide. It was established in 1882. Main production in the area came from the St. Jacobs Mine which is credited with production of over $1,000,000. A post office was in the area from 1889 to 1903. Most mines surrounding the town produced high grade silver, lead, copper, gold and zinc. The city actually sits one half on the Pacific side and the other half about a mile or two further up and over the divide on the Atlantic side. Some sources contend that the upper settlement is the City of Carson and the lower settlement was called Bachelor Cabins after the nearby Bachelor Mine. The Carson side trip should not be attempted in combination with the Ouray-Lake City round trip in a single day.

Returning to the main road, Mill Creek Campground is further upstream and a mile and a half beyond that point is the site of the former town of Sherman. The town was platted in 1877 and contained several stores, a sawmill, saloons, the Sherman House Hotel (which opened in 1881), and a large mill that dominated the town. A post office was operated from 1877 to 1898. The summer population probably reached a maximum of about 300 with only 40 or 50 hardy souls staying out the winter. The Black Wonder was the main mine in the area and it produced gold from copper pyrites and silver in ruby and brittle form. Most of the townsite has been obliterated by the flooding of Cottonwood Creek and the Lake Fork although the remains of several cabins are still visible. This very scenic valley is now the location of a campground and is also the turnaround point for conventional automobiles.

Journeying 6.6 miles further, one reaches Burrows Park from which excellent views of Red Cloud and Sunshine Peaks (both over 14,000 feet and favorite climbs) may be obtained. Within the valley's west end, all in a two-mile distance, were located the towns of Whitecross, Sterling, Argentum, Tellurium and a town called Burrows Park. Considerable confusion therefore exists as to the location of each. However, it is generally conceded that Argentum was located about November 1876 in the flat area north of Cooper Creek in the upper end of the Park. It had a hotel, two stores, a blacksmith shop and a post office as well as a dozen cabins. Burrows or Burrows Park were the names of a town in the general location of Argentum and may have actually been Argentum. It was composed of half a dozen cabins. The post office was changed from this name to Whitecross in 1882. Whitecross itself was established across the canyon from Whitecross Mountain. It was named for the white cross of quartz located in the knob on Whitecross Mountain, easily seen from the road. It was first located in 1880 and its peak population was probably about 300. Many men lived in or about the area and worked at the Tabasco Mill and Mine further up the road. Just a short distance above Whitecross was the "town" of Tellurim. By 1880, when Crofutt visited the town, it was already just "a small camp of a dozen persons." It was named for the gold-producing ore found in the San Juans. The cabins were scattered over a half a mile on both sides of the road. Also, above Whitecross was Sterling, which was probably little more than a tent city.

As the road steepens in its ascent of Cinnamon Pass, one passes by the ruins of the Tabasco Mill, its timbers spilled like jackstraws down the hillside. The mill was connected by an aerial tramway with the Tabasco Mine which is about two miles above and just past the crest of Cinnamon Pass. The mine and mill were owned by the Tabasco Sauce Company. The mill was built in 1901 and received its power from an electric plant in Sherman. It has a 100-ton capacity but operated for only four years.

From the top of Cinnamon Pass, at an elevation of 12,620 feet, a fine view can be had of 14,050-foot Handies Peak, with Redcloud Peak (14,017 feet) behind and Whitecross Mountain between the two. The road then descends into the valley of the Animas River and in 2.5 miles the site of Animas Forks (elevation 11,200 feet) is reached. A few houses, the unique wooden jail structure, and the foundations of the Gold Prince Mill are about all that remain to attest to the busy community that was the terminus of the Silverton Northern Railroad. That line was completed in 1904. The Gold Prince Mill, with 100 stamps, was Colorado's largest mill when it was built in Animas Forks in 1904 and was the state's first mill built of steel. Ore to feed it came by way of a long aerial tramway from the Gold Prince Mine. Among the remaining buildings is a gaunt, bay-windowed structure which some legends have it was once occupied by Tom Walsh before he struck it rich at the Camp Bird Mine above Ouray. However, there is no absolute proof of his occupancy. See Chapter 7 for more information on Animas Forks.

Silverton is reached by following the Animas River for 12 miles and, from there, roads lead to Ouray or Durango (See Chapter 7). The North Fork of the Animas can also be taken to Mineral Point and thence along the same route traversed at the start of this chapter to the Million Dollar Highway.

Animas Forks, now a ghost town, founded in 1875 and served by its own post office until 1915. The town, just at timberline, was the terminus of the Silverton Northern Railway. It is situated at the western base of Cinnamon Pass which divides the waters that flow into the Animas River on the west and the Lake Fork of the Gunnison River on the east. (Colorado Historical Society)

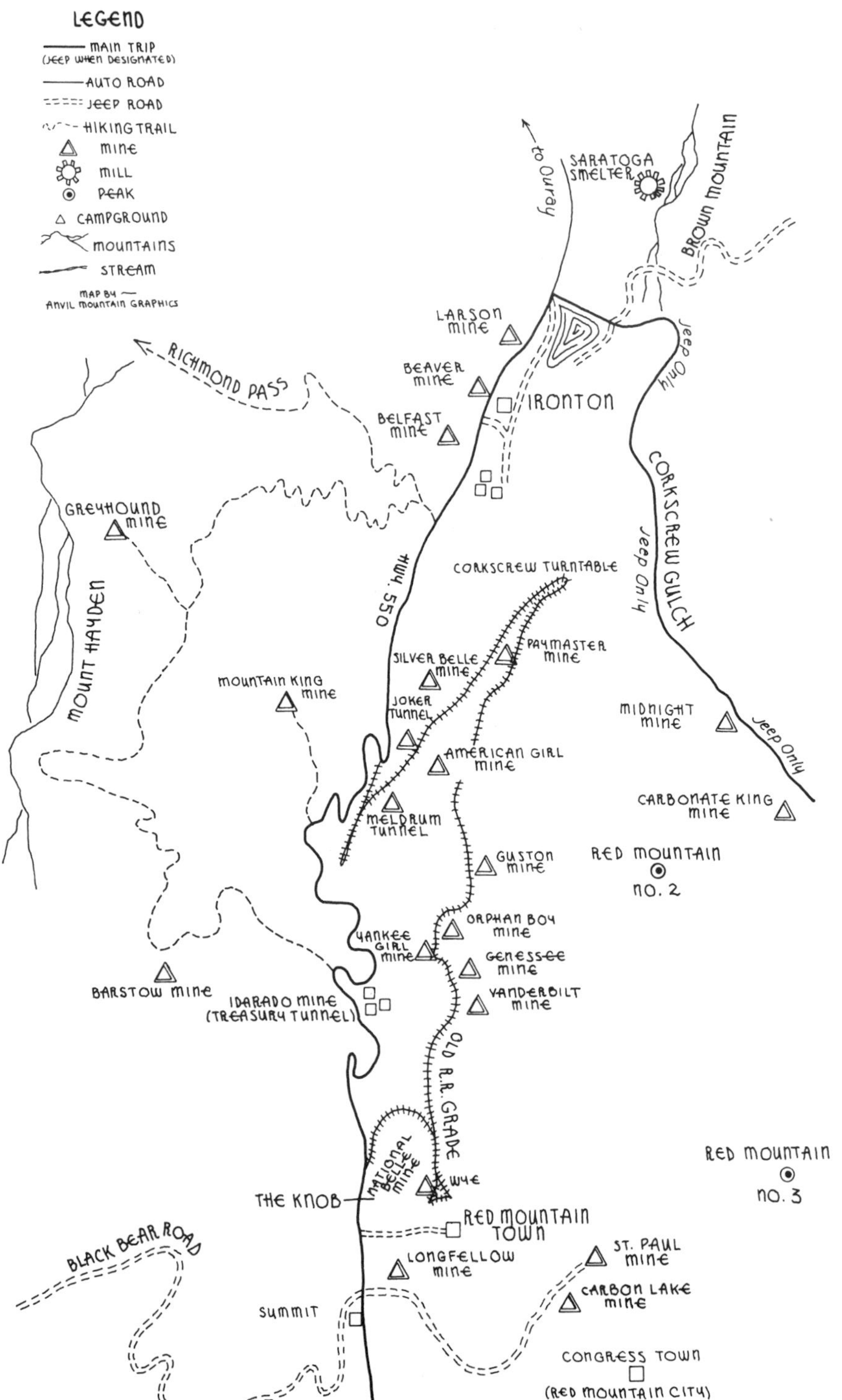

LEGEND

— MAIN TRIP
(JEEP WHEN DESIGNATED)
— AUTO ROAD
---- JEEP ROAD
~~~~ HIKING TRAIL
△ MINE
✿ MILL
◉ PEAK
△ CAMPGROUND
⌒⌒ MOUNTAINS
— STREAM

MAP BY —
ANVIL MOUNTAIN GRAPHICS

to Ouray

SARATOGA SMELTER

BROWN MOUNTAIN

RICHMOND PASS

LARSON MINE

BEAVER MINE

BELFAST MINE

IRONTON

Jeep Only

CORKSCREW GULCH

GREYHOUND MINE

HWY. 550

CORKSCREW TURNTABLE

MOUNT HAYDEN

MOUNTAIN KING MINE

SILVER BELLE MINE

PAYMASTER MINE

JOKER TUNNEL

MIDNIGHT MINE

AMERICAN GIRL MINE

CARBONATE KING MINE

MELDRUM TUNNEL

GUSTON MINE

RED MOUNTAIN NO. 2

YANKEE GIRL MINE

ORPHAN BOY MINE

GENESSEE MINE

BARSTOW MINE

IDARADO MINE (TREASURY TUNNEL)

VANDERBILT MINE

OLD R.R. GRADE

RED MOUNTAIN NO. 3

THE KNOB

NATIONAL BELLE MINE

WYE

RED MOUNTAIN TOWN

BLACK BEAR ROAD

LONGFELLOW MINE

ST. PAUL MINE

CARBON LAKE MINE

SUMMIT

CONGRESS TOWN
(RED MOUNTAIN CITY)

CHAPTER 6
Red Mountain
Cities of Silver

Ernest Ingersoll called them gaudier than a cardinal's hat. Frank Hall in his history of Colorado called them the Scarlet Peaks and reported that Professor Hayden says "they are due to admixtures of certain mineral substances." We call them Red Mountain.

Red Mountain is actually three mountains. The highly oxidized iron in the mountains makes them glow after rains. In certain light it is as if red or yellow paint had been poured down their sides. But it was something different the prospectors were after. The mountains' interiors contain a number of pipe-like areas of unbelievably rich silver-lead and silver-copper ores.

The Red Mountain mining district was first prospected in September 1879. Gold, silver, lead and copper were produced in the area. The **Red Mountain Pilot** of April 28, 1883 reported that there were:

"five towns in the district as follows: Chattanooga, eight miles from Silverton and D & RG Railroad; Red Mountain City, one mile distant (both of these towns are in San Juan County, the latter being about half a mile from the county line); Red Mountain, or Hudson Town is one mile from Red Mountain City, in Ouray County and half a mile from the county line; Rogerville is about half a mile from said Hudson Town; and Ironton is four miles distant from Hudson..."

Ironton was founded in 1883 and platted March 20, 1884. In March 1883, it had 32 cabins being built. It was the supply town for many rich mines in the area and later in 1889 the passenger terminus for the railroad. The 1890 census listed a population of 323. The town had its own water system, electric plant, post office, two churches and fire department. In the 1890s, the area began to wane with the fall in silver prices, but the discovery of small amounts of gold kept the area alive. People lived in the town proper until the 1960s. Today, only a half dozen houses still stand as most were torn down for their lumber.

Traveling further up Highway 550, the Silver Belle Mine is visible across the creek. It operated from 1880 to 1894, but became the first of the Red Mountain mines to have to shut down because of water, sulphuric acid and the high costs of the deep shafts following the volcanic pipes. It was one of the best producers in the area with ten levels and an output of over a million dollars mainly in silver. The Paymaster was located slightly above the Silver Belle. It produced $178,000 between 1887 and 1890.

The Joker Tunnel was located just above the Silver Belle. Its boardinghouse still stands by the road. Its purpose was to drain water

Ironton, looking north on Main Street. Probably at about the zenith of the town's boom for, despite some exaggerated claims, the largest census figure that we can find lists Ironton's population as 325 souls. Only a few of the town's buildings remain at the extreme southern end of the townsite. (Colorado Historical Society)

Overall view of Ironton, looking from south to north. The best picture we were able to find, but if one looks closely, most of the town can be made out. (Denver Public Library)

from the rich mines further to the south and allow economical mining at a lower level. George Crawford and C. H. Graham spearheaded its construction. It eventually extended 4,800 feet and allowed the area's mines to operate another decade.

The Meldrum Tunnel was located about 1,750 feet south of the Joker Tunnel. It was started by Andrew S. Meldrum, one of the original locators of the Yankee Girl and Guston mines. The Meldrum Tunnel was a great scheme, not with a purpose of connecting towns as some writers have surmised, but rather to permit the use of full-sized narrow gauge railroad cars to travel by tunnel to a point above Telluride, bringing back ore and switching directly onto the tracks of the Silverton Railroad. The bore from each end would have enough upward grade to provide drainage of the great quantities of water always encountered deep within the mountains. Ore chutes would have been tunneled into several of the big mines that were already operating at higher levels than the Meldrum Tunnel, thus providing much cheaper and more convenient transportation of their ores. It was also probable that in the construction of the tunnel, rich veins might be discovered which could be mined directly by way of the tunnel access.

Andy Meldrum had secured his capital from British investors, many of whom were already gleefully gambling on mining ventures in the San Juans. The project had only a fair beginning when the Boer War broke out in South Africa. The British money boys saw, perhaps, a quicker profit and more sport for the time being in financing a war. Meldrum's money source dried up and his dream ended with only about 800 feet completed at this end and 2,000 feet at the Telluride end. The company went bankrupt.

This Jackson photo, labeled "Red Mountain Mines," shows the camp that later became known as "Guston;" only a half mile from the platted townsite of Red Mountain Town and part of the "Red Mountain Precinct." Early census figures for Red Mountain Town also included the population of this camp. Most of the buildings in the foreground of this picture are of dwellings, those in back are of mines. The tall, slender structure, just left and slightly above center of this picture, is the shaft-house of the famous Yankee Girl Mine.
(Colorado Historical Society)

Traveling uphill past several switchbacks brings one to a spot where a road leads to the west up to the Mountain King Mine (also called Betsy and Gold Lion at earlier times). The vein is visible on the surface and runs some 6,000 feet down into Ironton Park. It has been prospected and worked off and on for years. Cave-ins were bad at the mine because the walls of the vein were heavily altered. The last big operations were in the middle 1940s.

For the next quarter mile, by looking across the canyon towards Red Mountain, a jumble of buildings are visible below Champion Gulch. Generally, this is what used to be the town of Guston which was made up of three very famous and large mines - from north to south, the Guston-Robinson, the Yankee Girl, and Genessee-Vanderbilt. Guston had a post office, but its pride and joy was its church. It was built by an Englishman, Rev. William Davis, in 1891. He did the work almost singlehandedly with the miners supplying lumber and money. Some of the congregation in the camp felt that a church was not a proper church without a bell. Consequently, a campaign was begun to raise funds for the purpose of adding a belfrey and installing a bell. As contributions were being solicited one Cornish miner, accustomed in the old country to timing all his daily activities by the toots of the mine whistle, thought he would prefer a whistle to a bell on the church. He offered to pay the cost of installing the whistle and steam line from a nearby boiler. If that was the way to get him into church on Sunday morning, it was done! A bell and a whistle were installed in the belfrey.

In 1888, several dozen houses had been erected and perhaps 200 people lived in the area. The town's streets were steep and snaked around the mountain, one above the other. By 1890, 332 persons were living in the town. However, by 1897, the mines had shut down and most future development came through the Joker Tunnel to the northwest.

The Guston Mine was located on August 21, 1881 by August Dietlat, Andrew Meldrum, John Robinson and Albert Lang. At first the mine was operated mainly for its lead. John Robinson later made the important discovery when he picked up a rock that turned out to be very heavy and broke it open to discover it was solid galena (a rich silver-lead ore). The Guston is believed by some to have produced close to $8,000,000. When the shaft was only 20 feet deep, the mine was sold for $125,000! Robinson then staked out the Robinson and Orphan Boy on adjoining land - both of which also proved to be equally valuable because of the huge ore deposits. Development was slow at first and it was not until 1888 that large scale production began. Some of the mine's hand-picked ore averaged 15,000 ounces of silver per ton with 3 ounces of gold. The Guston was developed on 14 levels to a depth of 1,300 feet. Not one Colorado mine in ten ever paid a cent of dividends to stockholders, but in the ten-year period between 1888 and 1897, the Guston was able to pay over one million dollars in dividends to its stockholders. The Robinson reportedly bottomed out at 600 or 700 feet.

The Yankee Girl Mine was only about 300 yards away from the Guston-Robinson and operated concurrently with the Guston for some time. It produced over $8 million during its time (over $6 million in the 1890s alone) and it was more famous than its sister mines. The Yankee Girl was staked August 19, 1882. The **Red Mountain Pilot** in its March 10, 1883 issue said that "the Yankee Girl is the mine that gave Red Mountain the boom. One month after it was located, Silverton parties paid $125,000

Another view of the Yankee Girl shaft-house and the power plant
(twin smokestacks). Tracks of the Silverton Railroad can be seen just
below the house at upper right. (Colorado Historical Society)

for it. This property includes half a dozen locations, two of which are the Orphan Boy and Robinson, which promise as well as the Yankee Girl...This mine was discovered last August, and up to the time of our visit, had produced $54,288..." The tower-like shaft house of the Yankee Girl is still highly visible from the road. The Mine was developed to a depth of 1,050 feet and produced very rich ore of up to 3,000 ounces of silver per ton with the added bonus of up to 30% copper. Once, a ten-ton ore car of picked and sorted mineral was sold for $75,000.

The Orphan Boy made up a part of the Yankee Girl group which was basically five "chimneys" of ore - Yankee Girl, Orphan Boy, North, West and South. There is some debate over the quality of the ore at the time the mine closed down. One source says the mine was down to low-grade pyrites and another says it was in a rich copper ore. At any rate, by 1897 operations had ceased. The mine had its own large powerhouse with two large smokestacks and an extremely attractive boardinghouse. Otto Mears was a part owner of the mine and a considerable amount of traffic over the Silverton Railroad was to and from this mine. Mears even went down several times to watch the mining so that he could tell the people to whom he gave his famous silver filigre passes that he had seen them from the raw material to the finished product. Ore from the Guston/Yankee Girl/Orphan Boy was so high grade it was shipped directly to the smelters without sorting. Quite a bit of low grade ore was just thrown on the dumps and was milled in the 1920s and 1930s at a profit by handsorting.

The Genessee-Vanderbilt was located slightly south of the Yankee Girl. The Genessee was discovered in 1882 by Jasper Brown and Adelbert Parsell. As was the case of most mines in the area, it also developed slowly. In 1889, it merged with the Vanderbilt. The Vanderbilt was also begun about 1882 and by the time of the merger it had only been developed to a small extent. Production was probably about $1 million. The ore was of a lower grade than the Yankee Girl and Guston-Robinson. However, the mine produced considerable silver, gold, lead and copper. It has a 4,500-foot tunnel and a 700-foot shaft with five levels. The mine was intensively worked in the 1940s and many of the buildings are still seen standing.

If one travels south on Highway 550 for a short distance, the road passes through the Idarado Mine's complex of mine buildings, warehouses and company houses. The mine has had a checkered career of operation, and represents a collection of many old mines in an attempt at a more economically sound effort. The area was first developed at an elevation of 10,620 feet as the Hammond Tunnel and then by the Treasury Tunnel Mining and Milling in about 1896. A side track was laid for the Silverton Railroad. For about ten years, operations continued, but then the area slumped. A big boardinghouse on the property was later torn down. The mine was then only worked a little until 1937 when San Juan Metals built a new mill, boardinghouse and other buildings.

At the beginning of World War II, the U.S. government instituted crash programs of all sorts to overcome the many deficiencies that were making it difficult to fight even a war of defense. Metals were greatly needed for the manufacture of war machines and supplies. The Treasury Tunnel was more or less preempted by the government which subsidized the drilling of tunnels to tap the Barstow, The Argentine, The Black Bear and other mines, all at higher levels than the Treasury Tunnel and whose potentials for good ores were well known. The Sunshine Mining Co. of Grass Valley California was given a contract for this rapid tunnel expansion program. They came into the area, bringing with them their own management, foremen, engineers and even some miners, though many local miners were also employed. In 1944-45, the Sunshine Mining Company's contract was completed and operation was taken over by the Idarado Mining Co., a newly formed subsidiary of the Newmont Corporation. In 1954, a fire destroyed a large part of the surface buildings but the company rebuilt. The mill operated continuously with an output of about 800 tons of ore per day. The dump expanded to fill a small pond (Malcom Lake) that used to be by the property, then down the mountainside to Ironton. Idarado eventually bought the Tomboy and other famous holdings near Telluride. In 1956, a new mill with 1800-ton capacity was built near Telluride and the mill on Red Mountain was shut down. It is possible to go through the workings to Telluride and all ore in recent years was brought out on that side. The mine has more than 80 miles of interconnected tunnels and joins the old workings of the Tomboy, Ajax, Smuggler, Liberty Bell, Virginius, Pandora, Japan, Barstow, Argentine, Black Bear, Wheel of Fortune and many more. The mine produced gold, silver, lead, copper and zinc.

At a hairpin curve a short distance above the Idarado, a road (usually closed and private property) leads to the northwest. This road leads to the Barstow Mine and then on to the Greyhound which has been previously discussed. The Barstow was originally called the Bobtail Mine. It is located in Commodore Gulch three quarters of a mile northwest of the Idarado. The mine operated from 1895 to 1918. For quite some time around the turn of the century, it was the only mine shipping ore from the Red Mountain area. It produced slightly less than a million dollars, chiefly in gold, silver, copper, lead, iron and zinc, with a production of fluorite during World War I. It has over 11,000 feet in tunnels. A large boardinghouse and mill were on the site in the early 1900s. The mill had forty stamps and two Wilfley tables. A short tram brought ore from the upper workings to the mill and a snowshed covered

Across Red Mountain Creek from the Guston Camp is the Treasury Tunnel, one of the many mines in the district. It was of average importance until World War II, when the U.S. Government sponsored the expansion of its already extensive workings to connect with several other large mines, mostly above and beyond. The result is a vast network of interconnected passageways, extending through the range to Pandora on the Telluride side and under the mountains to connect with the Revenue Mine in the Sneffels district. Renamed "Idarado," this great mine was the largest operation of its kind ever in the State of Colorado. Operations continued more than thirty-five years after the close of World War II. Terribly inflated operating costs and a poor metal market has compelled closure, it is hoped, only temporarily. (Denver Public Library)

the tracks from the lower level.

Shortly before reaching the top of Red Mountain Pass and a little over a mile above the Barstow cutoff, a small road leads to the left to Red Mountain Town and the National Belle Mine. Considerable confusion has existed because there were two towns called "Red Mountain." Muriel Wolle in her wonderful book **Stampede to Timberline** uses a quote from the Solid Muldoon of Ouray - January 19, 1883:

"'The Red Mountain Pilot' and 'Red Mountain Review' are both published in Silverton and are a tissue of falsehood. There is but one tent and three bunches of shingles in Red Mt. City, they blow so much about, and miners of Red Mt. refuse to patronize or tolerate such frauds. Both the enterprising editors have been ordered out of camp. Red Mt. needs neither gush nor exaggeration. We have enough ore in sight to attract capitalists and insure permanency and do not desire the services of journalists who are willing to do an unlimited amount of lying for a certain number of town lots. Curry and Raymond would kill any camp.''

The Barstow Mine in Commodore Gulch, west of the Treasury Tunnel. This mine, hidden from view from the highway, was first of the many mines to have been connected with the Treasury during World War II. (Denver Public Library)

The key to understanding the above paragraph is the use of the word "City" in the first mention of "Red Mt." and the subsequent use of Red Mt. without the added "City." Contemporary readers did not need further explanation for the intense rivalry between the papers of San Juan County and those of Ouray County was well understood. In 1883, Red Mountain City in San Juan County and Red Mountain Town in Ouray County were conversation topics in every saloon and barbershop and on every street corner. A careful re-reading of the quote from the "Red Mt. Pilot" at the beginning of the chapter illustrates this even more clearly. Mrs. Wolle incorrectly assumes that the "Muldoon" and the "Red Mt. Pilot" are talking about the same town, for she states that "in less than two months, however, the "Muldoon" admitted that progress had been made by printing the following paragraphs (again, note the absence of the word "City"):

"Five weeks ago the site where Red Mt. now stands was woodland mesa, covered with heavy spruce timber. Today hotels, printing offices, groceries, meat markets, a telephone office, saloons, dance houses are up and booming; the blast is heard on every side and prospectors can be seen snowshoeing in every direction.

"Everything has been packed or sledded over or under three feet of snow — We predict that by Sept. 1, Red Mt. will have a population of nearly ten thousand and a daily output surpassed by Leadville only."

Perhaps the prediction in the paragraph above also gave rise to later exaggerated claims of some scholars as to the population of Red Mountain Town and the district. Not in all its history is there any good

A winter view of Red Mountain Town, looking south toward the pass. This picture is obviously one taken following the first fire and after the town was partially rebuilt. (Ruth Gregory Collection)

Congress, the town that tried to become "Red Mountain City." Vying with Red Mountain Town for the right to the name, the U.S. Postal Department assigned the name "Congress," thus ending the contest. (Denver Public Library)

The Congress Mine, which supplied the name for the town which grew up near it and because of it. Thomas F. Walsh was part owner and general manager of the Congress at the same time that he was getting his great Camp Bird Mine in operation. (Ruth Gregory Collection)

Winter scene on the upper (east) side on Main Street, Red Mountain Town. The town was incorporated, had a water system but no sewers. The "outback" facilities were reached through tunnel-like snowsheds. There was no snowplowing, but pack animals, teams and cutters kept a pathway broken through the street. Such was life above 11,000 feet! (Denver Public Library)

evidence that at any one time there were ten thousand people in the entire of Ouray County, even when it included what are now Dolores and San Miguel counties.

Red Mountain Town was platted in the old conventional "grid" pattern — streets and avenues forming squares where they crossed. The site was about the only one in the region where such a town could have been built. The railroad was built to the town, not only to take advantage of the commerce the town would generate but to pick up the product of the National Belle Mine which was within the town.

During the period of rivalry between the two Red mountains, the editor of the "Red Mountain Pilot" exchanged insults with the "Solid Muldoon" week after week. The editor of the "Pilot" never had a good word for anything or anybody on the Ouray side of the county line. A plan to build a road from Red Mountain Town to connect with a road from Silverton up Cement Creek to Poughkeepsie was "no less than a scheme to turn traffic from towns in San Juan County into Ouray County." In the issue of March 31, 1883: "The people of Ouray are 'in earnest' and hope to get the trail from Ouray to Red Mountain in passable condition by the first of June." He didn't try to hide his bitterness after the Postal Department had designated Red Mountain City's post office as "Congress." Heretofore, he had always referred to Red Mountain Town as "Hudson" town. In a column headed "Local Laconics", he began with:

"CONGRESS
CONGRESS
CONGRESS
CONGRESS is our Post Office
CONGRESS is our address
Arrivals are increasing every day
The snow is disappearing rapidly
CONGRESS, San Juan County, Colorado!
We have a daily mail — Tom Williams carries it.
Another week will see a thousand more men in the district.
Half the population of Hudson Town (Red Mt. Town)
is sporting women and their pimps.
A good span of mules cannot pull an empty wagon over the range
from Silverton to Hudson Town (Red Mt. Town)
by the proposed Cement Creek route."

On May 19, 1883, the editor of the "Pilot" was complaining:
"A large number of our exchanges continue to address us as Red Mountain City and are carried by to Red Mountain Town and frequently lay there a week before the thick-headed postmaster sends them back...All our exchanges will please change their addresses to ' Congress, San Juan County ' and thus avoid delays."

With the imposed name change, Red Mountain City had lost out in the contest for the right to the permanent use of the name Red Mountain. By 1885, Red Mountain City (Congress) had a population of only 130 and by 1887, only a handful of people lived there. By 1890, Red Mountain Town, however, had a population of 598 with its own telephone office, two newspapers, schoolhouse, post office (it boasted "the highest in the world"), and many saloons. The town was plagued by fires - one major one on August 13, 1892 and another on June 13, 1895. Each destroyed over half the town despite the fact the town had its own waterworks and a very good volunteer fire department.

Rev. J.J. Gibbons reported in 1891 that:

"the lights never went out in the camp, unless when coal oil failed, or a stray cowboy shot up the town. The men worked night and day, shift and shift about and the people were happy. The gambling halls never closed. The restaurants did a profitable business, and no one could lay his weary bones on a bed for less than a dollar."

By 1893, the population had dropped to about 400 and in 1894, to 200. By 1899, the winter population was only 12 and in 1900, 30 people were there to be counted by the census, but they lived there only in the summer. Much of what remained of the town was destroyed in a forest fire in 1937. The jailhouse and a few mine buildings are about all that is left. The jail was made of tons of solid wood and was built on solid bedrock so no one could dig out.

The National Belle Mine was located in January 1883 within the city limits of Red Mountain on the big knob at the end of town. It was an early producer of soft carbonates, galena, and grey copper which were not very rich ($75 per ton or so) but which could be very easily and cheaply mined. Six months after it was located, the owners were offered $160,000 for the mine. It was in July 1883 that the big excitement happened. An immense cavern was discovered which was like a treasure cave - filled with pockets of gold and silver galena as well as chlorides and carbonates.

Ernest Ingersoll reported that:

"a workman broke through the walls into a cavity. Hollow echoes came back from the blows of his pick, and stones thrown were heard to roll a long distance. Taking a candle, one of the men descended and found himself in an immense natural chamber, the flickering rays of the light showing him the vaulted roof far above, seamed with bright streaks of galena and interspersed with masses of soft carbonates, chlorides and pure white talc. On different sides of this remarkable chamber were small openings leading to other rooms or chambers, showing the same rich formation. Returning from this brief reconnaissance a party began a regular exploration. They crept through the opening into an immense natural tunnel running above and across the route of their working drift for a hundred feet or more, in which they clambered over great bowlders (sic) of pure galena, and mounds of soft grey carbonates, while the walls and roof showed themselves a solid mass of chloride carbonate ores of silver. Returning to the starting point they passed through another narrow tunnel of solid and glittering galena for a distance of forty feet, and found indications of other large passages and chambers beyond...It would seem as though Nature had gathered her choice treasures from her inexhaustable storehouse, and wrought these tunnels, natural stopping places and chambers, studded with glittering crystals and bright mineral to dazzle the eyes of man in after ages, and lure him on to other treasures hidden deeper in the bowels of the earth."

The railroad yards at Red Mountain Town. Bottom, foreground is the depot astride Red Mountain Creek (the creek actually flowed under the building). The two "wyes" made it possible to turn the train around without uncoupling the engine or using a turntable. High on the hill at right is the National Belle Mine; the small building, just beyond the freight cars at left, is the city jail. Above the jail is one of the main street buildings; anything on the other side of the street that might have been in view is obscured by the two trees at left.
(Denver Public Library)

People came from miles around to gawk at the treasure cave. The main cave was 200 feet in length and 100-feet wide. Within a week another even larger mineral cave was discovered. The **Red Mountain Pilot** reported (7/21/83) "No where else in the world is there such a large body of mineral as there is in the National Belle and no one knows the extent of the mineral there is at least a million tons in sight and no one can estimate the value...One of the best features about this rich discovery is that the present owners were original locators and they will reap the fruits of their toil instead of some tin-horn capitalist."

The mine became one of the best known in the country and produced almost $9,000,000. The shaft house still stands above the dump and loading chutes. At first the mine produced huge quantities of up to 60% lead but, then as production grew deeper, copper of up to 40% was found. By 1897, the mine closed after being developed to a depth of 450 feet.

Across to the west of 550, a pack trail leads north and west up to Ptarmigan Lake and Senator Beck Mine. This used to be called "The High Line Trail" and hundreds of tame ptarmigan could be found along the way. Today, both sides of the highway provide access to good cross-country skiing.

About half a mile further south on Highway 550 is Red Mountain Pass summit. The sign reads elevation 11,018 feet but its actual elevation is 11,075 feet. This is the county line between Ouray and San Juan. It is also the division between the San Juan and Uncompahgre forests and the Uncompahgre and Animas River Watershed. The sign reads "Gold ore wagons first passed here in 1878" but it was actually later in 1882 before any roads were built. The railroad used to follow the road from this point south. Red Mountain was the highest railroad pass in the U.S. when the

Silverton Railroad was built in 1887. The crest was named "Summit" by the railroad.

The train at the highest point on the "Rainbow Route." It is now known as "Red Mountain Pass," but in railroad days was called "Summit," and also "Sheridan Junction." Although Sheridan Junction never made any pretense of being a town (it never had a post office, being within a half-mile walking distance to Red Mountain Town), it did have the Sheridan Hotel. (Denver Public Library)

The early ore processing mills were known as "stamp mills." A stamp consisted of a heavy vertical steel rod, weighing several hundred pounds, fitted with a "shoe" of very tough metal at the bottom and a concave "anvil" beneath the shoe. Near the top of the rod was a collar, by which means the cams shown in this picture were able to lift the rod several inches then allow it to drop of its own weight, pulverizing ore that had already been reduced to a small gravel. Actually a huge, mechanical adaptation of the simple mortar and pestle. (Bill Fries III)

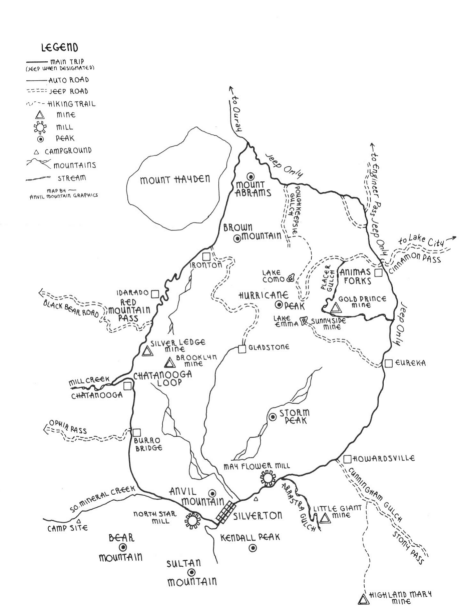

LEGEND

— MAIN TRIP
(JEEP WHEN DESIGNATED)
—— AUTO ROAD
===== JEEP ROAD
∿∿∿ HIKING TRAIL
△ MINE
✺ MILL
⊙ PEAK
△ CAMPGROUND
⩗ MOUNTAINS
— STREAM

MAP BY
ANVIL MOUNTAIN GRAPHICS

to Ouray

Jeep Only

to Engineer Pass Jeep Only

MOUNT HAYDEN

MOUNT ABRAMS

POUGHKEEPSIE GULCH

BROWN MOUNTAIN

to Lake City

IRONTON

LAKE COMO

PLACER GULCH

ANIMAS FORKS

CIMARRON PASS

IDARADO

RED MOUNTAIN PASS

BLACK BEAR ROAD

HURRICANE PEAK

GOLD PRINCE MINE

Jeep Only

LAKE EMMA

SUNNYSIDE MINE

SILVER LEDGE MINE

BROOKLYN MINE

GLADSTONE

EUREKA

MILL CREEK

CHATANOOGA LOOP

CHATANOOGA

OPHIR PASS

STORM PEAK

BURRO BRIDGE

MAY FLOWER MILL

HOWARDSVILLE

CUNNINGHAM GULCH

SO. MINERAL CREEK

ANVIL MOUNTAIN

ABRASTRA GULCH

LITTLE GIANT MINE

STONY PASS

NORTH STAR MILL

SILVERTON

CAMP SITE

BEAR MOUNTAIN

KENDALL PEAK

SULTAN MOUNTAIN

HIGHLAND MARY MINE

CHAPTER 7
Red Mountain, Silverton and Animas Forks
Follow the Rainbow

This journey largely follows the pioneer paths of early railroads from the top of Red Mountain Pass to Silverton (the Silverton Railroad), thence northeast along the Animas River to Howardsville, Eureka, and Animas Forks (the Silverton Northern). Both narrow gauge routes were built by the master road and railroad builder, Otto Mears. The Silverton was begun in 1887 and completed in 1888. It was nicknamed "The Rainbow Route" — probably because of the arched path it made over Red Mountain Pass with a pot of gold at the end. Most of the road can easily accommodate any passenger car, the section on U.S. Highway 550 between Red Mountain and Silverton being paved and of moderate grades, while the portion from Silverton to Animas Forks is mostly a good gravel road (going into a somewhat rougher and steeper section between Eureka and Animas Forks that is somewhat questionable in a low slung car).

Starting atop Red Mountain Pass, the elevation is 11,075 feet. As the highway descends, the view down Mineral Creek includes the headframe and dump of the Silver Ledge Mine, started in 1883. The original vein contained huge amounts of silver. The March 3, 1883 "Red Mountain Pilot" reported that Chattanooga was thrown into a fever by the discovery and that it was the largest body of ore the editor has seen. The road then enters the Chattanooga Loop which was just one of many engineering feats of Charles W. Gibbs. The railroad curve at Chattanooga Loop (also called Muleshoe Curve) was 200 degrees, encompassing a climb of 550 feet in a quarter-mile. In the valley beyond the curve are the remains of the town of Chattanooga. The view ahead toward Silverton is dominated by Bear Mountain, so named because of the profile created by trees showing a bear with upraised paws holding a honeycomb.

Chattanooga was founded in March 1883. It was a good example of how rapidly and efficiently the U. S. Postal Service could act in those days. Mail was carried on men's backs, on pack animals, in hacks and stagecoaches, and trains powered with coal-burning locomotives. Yet within thirty days of its founding, Chattanooga had its post office established on April 3, 1883. By the middle of May of the same year, the town already contained seventy-five buildings in various stages of construction — including a hotel, two general stores, two bakeries, two drug stores, two meat markets, a blacksmith shop, restaurants and saloons. The town was partially destroyed in 1888 by a snowslide and a fire in 1892 finished off most of what remained. The town's peak had been in the mid-1880s before the coming of the railroad diminished its usefulness as a supply town.

Chattanooga before the coming of the railroad and before the fire that destroyed the town. Bear Mountain is seen at the end of the valley (bear silhouette is formed by timber). (Ruth Gregory Collection)

The highway follows Mineral Creek past its confluence with Mill Creek to reach a turnoff to the east. The new road leads up the mountain to the Brooklyn Mine. Continuing along the road a bit farther, on a turnoff to the west, is the location of Burro Bridge (an early-day settlement of a dozen cabins). This is the start of the four-wheel-drive road that leads over Ophir Pass to the towns of Old Ophir and New Ophir on the Howard Fork of the San Miguel River. The Ophir Pass Road was originally a wagon toll road, opened in 1881 to carry ore from Ophir to the mill in Silverton. It is now one of the easier four-wheel-drive roads in the area.

Another five miles brings the traveler to Silverton where the "Rainbow Route" met the trackage of the Silverton Northern, the Silverton Gladstone and Northerly, and the Denver and Rio Grande. The first three of the four railroads were abandoned 20 to 40 years ago. What used to be the D & RG is the only one still operating. It is, in fact, the last narrow gauge railroad in the United States still operating on a daily schedule under approval of the Interstate Commerce Commission. The railroad is a tourist run between Durango and Silverton.

The area in which Silverton is now located was first called Baker's Park after Capt. Charles Baker who first led a party of miners from Leadville to prospect the area in 1860. The July 22, 1882 **La Plata Miner** recounted Mr. Frank Koerle's recollections of the Baker party:

"There were about 150 men in the party. They built a bridge across the San Juan River at Pagosa Springs, also one across the Pine River; in fact, nearly all the larger

Looking down Mineral Creek from a point on the Silverton Railway on the southern approach to Red Mountain Pass. On the valley floor at lower left, the tracks of the Silverton Railroad approach the grade up the pass. They make a minor bend to the right, then a much more pronounced loop to the left leading to the very tight "Chattanooga Loop" (also known as "Muleshoe Curve") from which point the train climbed 500 feet in a quarter mile. A few scattered buildings on the valley floor (center) are the remains of Chattanooga, a bustling town of 300 population in toll road days and before the coming of the railroad. (Colorado Historical Society)

Silver Ledge Mine on upper Mineral Creek, just below Red Mountain Pass. Ore was transported to a railway loading station at Chattanooga by aerial tramway. (Ruth Gregory Collection)

streams were bridged. When they came to Cascade Creek they ascended it to its head and came down Bear Creek to its junction with Mineral Creek, and encamped at the lower end of the park. This was in September. Up to the time they encamped on Mineral Creek they had seen no Indians but Mr. Koerle says the next morning it seems as if there was an Indian behind every rock and tree on the mountainsides, and that the park was literally covered with them. The Indians forbade the party prospecting and told them to move on. [Koerle] says all the members of the party had had their hair cropped close, and that the Indians would come up to them, lift their hats, see the scarcity of hair, and say significantly 'Ugh! No buena!' It was here that the Indians brought in two captive children, which they sold to Colonel Pfieffer for five sacks of flour. The party came into the country well-equipped and supplied with provisions, and that Tom Pollock had several wagons drawn by ox teams, loaded with supplies. This fact caused their progress to be very slow, owing to the necessity of building bridges and chopping down trees...Afterwards being disappointed in not finding rich placers, as they had anticipated, the party broke up and scattered in all directions.''

The July 4, 1882 **La Plata Miner** recounted this important story:

''Later [Dempsey Reese (Silverton's First Mayor)] having been interested in and assisted in fitting out the...Baker's party and knowing from the reports of the survivors of that outfit of the wonderful richness of the mines, started from Arizona in 1869, and reached the lower Animas the latter part of that season, too late to get to the point they started before winter set in. They retraced their steps and wintered in Santa Fe, and early the next season Reese, Adrier French - since dead - and Cooley, prospected extensively and took a large quantity of specimens to Santa Fe for assay. Finding the majority of the specimens were rich, Reese and French with six others returned to the Animas in the spring of 1871 and commenced work on the Little Giant, packing tools, powder and provisions on burros for summer use. They built a Mexican arrastra and worked it during the season to good advantage. Out of the first six tons of quartz they cleared upwards of $300, occupying about six weeks in building the arrastra, mining quartz and grinding it out.

''The arrastra was run by water power and the entire building and manufacturing operations were performed with a hand ax, a plane, a chisel and an inch auger...The total product of the gold by this party, during the season, was in the neighborhood of $3,000. At the close of this season, the pioneer party broke up, some going to the States and others to Santa Fe to winter.

''From 1869 to 1873 the early settlers and prospectors labored under great pressure. Baker's Park being on the Ute reservation, they did not know what day or hour they would be driven out, either by the Indians or the United States Government. They labored on all this time, oppressed by anxiety and doubt as to what the future would

The village of Howardsville in 1875, then the county seat of La Plata County. Legend has it that the seat of county government was "abducted" and moved to Silverton. (The story is probably true since, when San Juan County was carved from La Plata County on January 31, 1876, Silverton automatically became the county seat as it was already there.) The one-room, log La Plata County Courthouse was also "abducted" in recent years and is one of the historic displays, just off Blair Street in Silverton. (Colorado Historical Society)

Street scene in Silverton in the 1880s. Looking south, Sultan Mountain forms the very scenic backdrop for this picture which appears to have been taken early in the day before the street was filled with people. All the rigs in view appear to be delivery wagons. (Ruth Gregory Collection)

be. They did not dare build a cabin or raise a roof, but were forced to sleep under trees or huts made of spruce boughs, with wet blankets and clothing.

"In the country there were no trails, no roads, no depots of supplies, and what was done was performed under difficulties that would have appalled ordinary men. The Indians were more considerate than the government, for they did not make any attempt to remove the settlers, while the government did.

"In June 1874 a town company was organized for the purpose of entering land for a townsite under the general act of Congress. The persons composing this company were Dempsey Reese, F.M. Snowden, Thomas Blair, N.E. Slaymaker, W. J. Mulholland, K. Benson and Samuel Champlin.

"Subsequently the smelting firms of Geo. Greene and Co. and Calder, Rouse & Co. were added to the company. Dempsey Reese was chosen President and N. E. Slaymaker, Secretary and Treasurer.

"The land covering the proposed townsite had previously been taken up as homestead by Mr. Reese, who built a house and fences, and held the land until the organization of the company, and the necessary application could be made. At the organization of the company there was not a single building on the present site (Reese's building being north of Cement Creek) and it was not until August that Thomas Blair built a dwelling house...

"The second building was a residence by N. E. Slaymaker known for a long time as the "Brown Stone Front." Its picturesque location and architectural appearance rendered it one of the principal attractions of the town in the early days. During the latter part of the season a half dozen other buildings for various purposes were erected, and Silverton began to assume the proportion of a town. At the general election the county seat of La Plata County was removed from Howardsville, where it had been located by an act of the legislature, creating the county to the new town. Greene & Co. started a new saw mill on Mineral Creek at the southern extremity of the park, and a smelter on Cement Creek, at the north end of town; they made one run, which showed that there was abundance of precious metal in the ore, although the process first adopted was defective...

"Several families came into the park during 1874 and located for the season at different points; upwards of 50 persons wintered this side of the range, consisting partly of the familiies of H. L. Rogers, W. E. Earl, Geo. Walz, John L. Lambert and Edward Greene. Provisions became very scarce before spring and much suffering ensued in consequence of sufficient calculation not having been made for the length and severity of the winter. It should be stated that during the previous winter four persons...had taken a contract on the Little Giant Mine Arrastra Gulch; they worked all winter, going down to the Animas Valley once on a visit for a few days.

"In the spring of 1875 prospectors and miners began to cross the range in March and the town received large accessions to its population, consisting of miners, mine owners and business men. Several dwellings and business houses were erected but owing to the scarcity of lumber, the number was limited."

Looking north on Silverton's main street in the mid-1880s. (The Grand Imperial Hotel at left was built in 1882.) (Ruth Gregory Collection)

Some of Silverton's structures have been well-maintained over the years. The most prominent buildings in present-day Silverton include the Grand Imperial Hotel, built in 1883, the San Juan County courthouse and the Congregational Church. Tourism and the large Sunnyside Mine have been the major contributors to the town's economy. The ore from the Sunnyside is milled in the Mayflower Mill just northeast of Silverton. This mill was originally built to serve the Mayflower and Shenandoah Dives mines in Arrastra Gulch and to do custom milling. It is not unusual for the Sunnyside operation to produce gold ore worth in excess of $50 million a year!

The American Tunnel (formerly known as the Standard Metals Mine) at Gladstone is a comparatively recent development. It was opened in the late 1950s by "Standard Uranium Corp." which was founded by Charlie Steen and a partner by the name of McCormick. Charlie Steen was the "Midas" of the Uranium boom in the earlier part of the same decade. Overnight, he went from an impoverished geologist and prospector to the possessor of more money than he could count - due to his discovery of the famous Mi Vida Mine near Moab, Utah.

The purpose of the American Tunnel was to bore into the mountain beneath the lowest workings of the fabulous Sunnyside Mine which had operated on the other side of the mountain at Eureka on the Animas River. The Sunnyside had closed down in the early forties for several reasons. First of all, the principal ore being mined was gold and gold mining was discouraged during World War II. Mining was then directed to lead, copper, zinc, and silver which were needed for the manufacture of war machines and materials. Secondly, the mine was being worked at levels well below the main haulage drifts which made it necessary to

The Sunnyside Mine, high above Eureka. Ore was conveyed to the big mill in Eureka via a long tramway. Lake Emma, partially visible in foreground, no longer exists since miners worked too close to its bottom, loosening the "plug" that gave way, letting the lake's waters flood down through all the workings underneath. The disaster occurred during a time when there was no one in the mine. Fortunately, there was no loss of life, but the destruction was so great that more than a year of cleanup was required before the mine could be operated again. (Ruth Gregory Collection)

Eureka, about 1917. The great Sunnyside Mill, built up the slope of the mountain, overlooks the town which had a lot of vitality in the early years of this century. The baseball teams of Ouray, Telluride and Silverton, challenging Eureka's teams, often wished that they had stayed home. (Ruth Gregory Collection)

hoist all the ore to those higher levels as well as to continually pump water from the lower workings. The American Tunnel, some six hundred feet below the lowest of the Sunnyside workings, by means of a "raise" at the proper point would drain all those old shafts, long filled with great quantities of water, dry up those rich ore bodies and the ore could be brought down by means of gravity (which is free) instead of the expensive method of hoisting.

Just past the Mayflower Mill, on State Highway 110 east of Silverton, the Arrastra Gulch road turns south across the Animas River. Four-wheel-drive is recommended and many of the mines can only be reached on foot. Three aerial tramways brought out ore or concentrates and carried in supplies to the Shenandoah Dives, the Silver Lake, and the Iowa-Royal Tiger mines. Towers and cables of two of these are still in place. Because no roads reach them, the machinery and buildings of these mines are more intact than most of the local mines that have been abandoned for that length of time.

Beyond the Arrastra turnoff, five miles east of Silverton, are the remains of Howardsville, containing some old buildings and a few new ones. When La Plata County was created in 1874, Howardsville was the county seat and the county was comprised of what are now La Plata, San Juan, Montezuma, Dolores, San Miguel and all that part of Ouray County not then part of the Indian reservation. Later, Silverton began to grow in size and importance and, as was not an uncommon occurrence in the Old West, the county seat was "pirated" one night and moved - books, inkwells, blotters and all - to that place. When San Juan County was cut out of La Plata County on January 31, 1876, Silverton remained the seat of the new county.

Closeup of the Sunnyside Mill at Eureka. The concrete foundations
on the mountainside are all that remain of this once great ore-mill.
(Colorado Historical Society)

Gold Prince Mill at Animas Forks. This was the first large mill in
the region to have been framed with structural steel. After only a few
short years the mill was dismantled, moved to Eureka and the
materials used in the building of the big Sunnyside Mill. Some cars
of the Silverton Northern Railway may be seen in the bottom of this
picture. Because of the steep grade, the engines pushed the cars
from Eureka to Animas Forks, but preceded them on the down trip;
this was because of the possibility of a coupling breaking and letting
loose a runaway car to come crashing into Eureka—if it stayed on the
rails that far! (Ruth Gregory Collection)

Howardsville is at the juncture of Cunningham Creek and the Animas River. It is also at the intersection of two roads, one following the Animas to Eureka, Animas Forks and Mineral point and the other being the old route up Cunningham Gulch and over Stony Pass to the headwaters of the Rio Grande, thence to Del Norte in the San Luis Valley.

Northeast of Howardsville, towards Animas Forks, the highway enters a wide portion of the valley where Eureka Gulch joins the Animas River. This was the site of the town of Eureka. Here, the Sunnyside Mine was largely responsible for the town's existence and it was in Eureka that the Sunnyside's mills were built. Eureka's post office was established on August 9, 1875 and was in continuous operation until May 1942. Eureka was incorporated in 1883 and had churches, a school, and sizeable residential and commercial districts.

The road up Eureka Gulch (which is for four-wheel-drive vehicles only) leads to the site of the Sunnyside Mine at 12,300 feet elevation. Originally, many surface buildings, including a boardinghouse, clustered around Lake Emma. Today, the buildings are gone and so is Lake Emma. In 1978, a stope in the mine caved in and drained the contents of the lake through its workings, out the portal at Gladstone, and down Cement Creek and the Animas River. It took more than two years of work before the mine could be operated again.

Sunnyside was discovered in 1873 and between 1917 and 1948 about 2½ million tons of ore, with a gross metal value of about $50 million, was produced. A 500-ton mill constructed in Eureka in 1917 was the first commerical lead-zinc selective flotation plant in North America.

Three miles north of Eureka over a somewhat rougher road is Animas Forks, which was transformed from a tent city to a town of substantial structures in 1877. It had its own post office, grade school and a wooden jail. A bay-windowed building, which is still standing, was reportedly once occupied briefly by Thomas F. Walsh of Camp Bird fame, but little evidence confirms the legend.

Remaining also is the foundation of a 100-stamp mill built for the Gold Prince Mine in 1907. It was Colorado's largest concentrating mill. The railroad, built in 1904 from Eureka to Animas Forks, followed an extremely steep grade - so steep that only a few cars could be pushed up the slope at one time. The Silverton Northern branch from Eureka to Animas Forks lasted only from 1904 to 1916, but even if its short life and short route did not merit it, it traveled in style. The dining car "Animas Forks" offered a menu and a wine list that would have held their own with those of the "20th Century Limited." And the cost of a full meal would not have paid the tip for a diner patron on Amtrak. Service, as far as Eureka, lasted until 1939 when the last concentrates were hauled from the Sunnyside Mill.

In 1917, only 10 years after being built, the Gold Prince Mill was dismantled and usable materials hauled to Eureka to build a new mill for the Sunnyside Mine. Workings of the Gold Prince were located at the head of Placer Gulch at 12,200 feet. A four-wheel-drive road, starting up California Gulch to the left from Animas Forks and forking again to the left beyond Bagley Tunnel, leads up Placer Gulch to the mine (formerly known as the Sunnyside Extension). A two-mile aerial tramway connected the mine with the mill. Although the area's surface structures gradually disappeared with the demise of various mines, revival of mining in the labrynth of underground workings has meant that gold production is alive and well in San Juan County.

The roads beyond Animas Forks go three ways, all for four-wheel-drive only. To the left, the road up California Gulch crosses Hurricane Pass, down to Lake Como. On down Poughkeepsie Gulch, the road is impassable. The center road goes up to Mineral Point near the base of Engineer Mountain and then either to the right over Engineer Pass to Lake City or to the left down Mineral Creek and the Uncompahgre River to Highway 550 (and eventually to Ouray). The third road to the right goes over Cinnamon Pass and on down the valley to Lake City. (See Chapter 5 for all three trips.)

Some segments of jeep roads above timberline must, of necessity, cross over talus beds. Talus is shale-like flakes of volcanic rock that is formed in a continuing process of freezing and thawing; talus is being produced all the time. Driving in some of these areas requires strict attention to business. Leaving the established tracks and driving onto sloping talus could provide a long ride down slope in moving rock with the possibility of jeep and occupants being buried under tons of shale. (Bill Fries III)

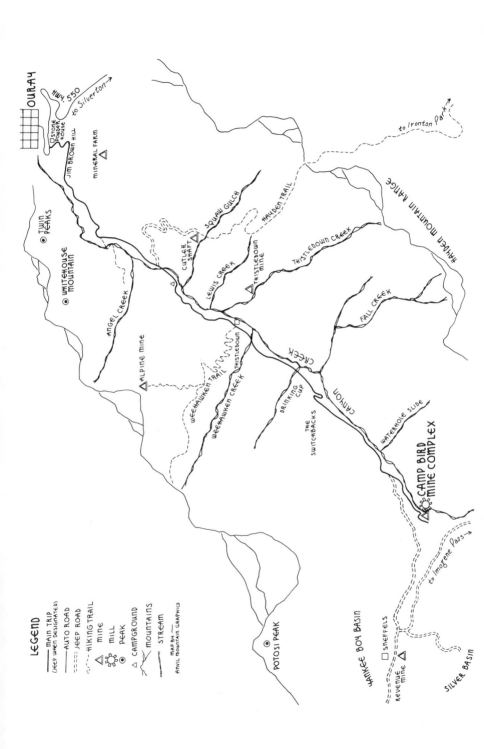

CHAPTER 8
Camp Bird
The Road to Riches

The Camp Bird Road now carries the name of one of Colorado's most famous mines. It was one that provided great wealth to the family of Tom Walsh. His daughter, Evalyn, lived high and spent millions during her lifetime. She wrote of her family's fortunes and misfortunes in her book "Father Struck It Rich."

Beginning in 1876, four attempts were made to construct the road before Otto Mears finally succeeded in 1881. Starting just south of the City of Ouray, an all-weather automobile road (Colorado 361) now follows Canyon Creek to the Camp Bird Mine and then fragments into several four-wheel-drive roads that lead into the high basins of Yankee Boy, Governor and Imogene. (See Chapters 9 and 10). These basins were the sites of such wealthy mining ventures as the Camp Bird, Virginius, Revenue and Ruby Trust.

In the early 1900s, at the zenith of mining in the area, it was reported that the Canyon Road was lined with horse-drawn wagons, mules and pack burros freighting in supplies and freighting out ore in an unbroken procession twenty-four hours a day. John Ashenfelter's teams of six huge horses would strain up the grades with drivers often strapped into their seats to keep from falling out. On the way down, the back wheels were fitted with "rough-locks," a device into which the iron tire on a rear wheel could be cradled and skidded on the steeper grades. The contrivance was forged of heavy iron, attached to a chain leading forward and then to a ring on the underside of the wagon. On the underpart of the rough-lock were sharpened "dogs" or "claws" that could bite into the roadbed. On roads that were "slanty," so that the wagon tended to skid to the low side, the rough-lock could be applied to the high wheel only which had the effect of making it skid in the opposite direction or, at least, keeping it in place.

Today there is a steady stream of four-wheel-drive vehicles bound for the high, cool meadows, the midsummer sea of wildflowers growing in the alpine basins and the hundreds of cascading waterfalls of pure melted snow.

To reach the road, leave Ouray on Highway 550 headed south, round the first hairpin turn, depart to the right, keep to the left through the highway department grounds, then cross the Uncompahgre Gorge. This marks the start of the climb up Jim Brown Hill which was named for a dairyman who lived in the area where the highway department shops are now located. The top of this hill affords an excellent view of the City of Ouray and the Amphitheatre with its colorful cliffs.

Just beyond the city's water tank a road forks to the left. This was once the access to the Mineral Farm Mine which was one of Ouray's earliest

Mule train, loaded with pipe, bound for one of the mines not reached by wagon road. Loads were always balanced with equal weight on either side of the animal and just enough weight, as with the pipe, to make it trail behind. This kept the cargo from swinging and possibly throwing the mule off balance. (Ruth Gregory Collection)

Freight wagon train on the Sneffels Road. These were always powered by no fewer than six sturdy, muscular horses and sometimes more. (Ruth Gregory Collection)

Mineral Farm Mine + Mill 1900

The Mineral Farm Mine and Mill, about 1900. Outcroppings of ore-bearing rock appeared haphazardly all over the level-to-sloping terrain so that it appeared it might be "harvested" right on the surface—hence the name "Mineral Farm." Never was there a continuous vein discovered; the ore was found in "pockets" and when a pocket was cleaned out, that's all there was until another pocket was found. One of the first mines staked in the area of Ouray, it was discovered by A.W. (Gus) Begole who was one of the first two prospectors known to enter this region. Begole was the only owner ever to realize any real profit from the Mineral Farm—when he sold it for $75,000. (Denver Public Library)

operations, having been discovered in the fall of 1875. The property today is not accessible to the public. The shallow trench-like diggings led to the mine's name as the gold and silver-bearing quartz could be harvested much as potatoes in a field. John Eckles and August W. Begole worked the mine until October 1878 when it was sold for $75,000. The **Ouray Times**, in its December 14, 1878 issue, excitedly reported that:

> "The transfer makes an epic in the history of mining in this section and ushers in the dawn of prosperity for our town and people. Business will undoubtedly be better and money more plentiful this winter than ever before in the history of the time, and we may congratulate ourselves that a company of such magnitude and with all so business-like in its management, has cast its lot in our community."

A variety of minerals were mined including ankerite, barite, chalcopyrite, copper and galena. For several years, in the decade of the 1930s, the Mineral Farm was still employing 30 to 40 men under the management of William (Bill) Cutler. Total production was valued at approximately one million dollars.

Just over a mile from town the canyon opens to provide a view of United States Mountain which cradles a huge snowfield (and correspondingly an avalanche area) most of the year and dominates the view of the canyon. The mountain takes its name from the U.S. Depository Mine located midway up its slope. At its base is the portal and mill of the Camp Bird Mine.

About a mile and a half from town a four-wheel-drive road turns sharply to the left and ascends two miles to the head of the Hayden Trail. At the end of the public portion of the road, and slightly beyond the trail head, is the headframe of the Culter Shaft, connected by a now collapsed tunnel to the Camp Bird Road. The mine operated briefly in the 1930s. The Hayden Trail leaves the road to the left and is a steep, rough foot trail that leads five miles over the top of Mt. Hayden and then descends to Ironton Park on the Million Dollar Highway . (See Chapter 4).

Directly across the Canyon Creek Bridge on the north of the Camp Bird Road is a small campground and trail which leads about one-half mile back to the Angel Creek area (originally called "Quaking Asp Flats"). Much of this area is private property although some camping is allowed. As one continues up the Camp Bird Road, several gulches (all avalanche areas) are visible to the left. The first is Squaw Gulch, so named since the large spire rising to the upper right of the gulch looks like a squaw carrying a papoose. The second gulch contains Lewis Creek and in the third, Thistledown Creek flows down the left side of the canyon. At this point a power pole can be spotted at the very top of Hayden Mountain which helped bring electricity to the area from Telluride.

About a half mile after crossing Canyon Creek a two-story, frame building will be seen on the left. This was the boardinghouse for the Thistledown Mine whose other buildings are visible among the aspen groves part way up the opposite slope. The mine, discovered in the early 1900s by M. L. Thistle, was a well financed project with a tram, mill, boardinghouse and even its own hydroelectric power; but it proved uneconomical. It was reopened for a short time after World War I to mine Fluorspar. Across the Camp Bird Road from the boardinghouse is the head of Weehawken Trail which provides an easy climb of several miles,

Thistledown Mill, bottom of picture. The mine is difficult to see in this picture; it is located on the first ledge above the snowy slope and to the left. This mine was operated chiefly for a soapy-looking, translucent, greenish-to-purple mineral known as "fluorspar," which is used as a flux in metallurgy and in the making of hydrofluoric acid, opal glass and some enamels. (Denver Public Library)

including a fork to the right which leads to the Alpine Mine and a fork to the left which travels high up Potosi Mountain. However, maintenance of the trail has been poor for the last few years and caution is advised.

Approximately two-tenths of a mile and beyond Weehawken Creek, a series of switchbacks carries the road along high shelves where it traverses cliffs at hundreds of feet above the canyon floor. At one point a

Thomas F. Walsh, discoverer and developer of the great Camp Bird Mine. Since he had no partners and sold no stock, all profits accrued to him alone. The Camp Bird Mine was the biggest, richest gold mine in the world to be owned by a single individual, hence the great fortune that was his in so short a time. (Colorado Historical Society)

small stream gushes year-round from a small crack in the rock above. Until a few years ago, when some of the rock was blasted away, the rock projected out over the road a bit. A large funnel was suspended from the rock and a hose led from the spout to the side of the road. In earlier times, the great wagons with their six-horse teams plying the road could stir up a lot of dust. Spikes were driven into small cracks in the rock near this upside down spring. Tincups were kept hanging on the spikes so that the wagon drivers might pause for a good, cold drink of delicious spring water and at the same time clear the dust from their throats. From then until now, the place carries the name "Drinking Cup."

At the end of the shelf, the road and stream are at nearly the same level. The canyon narrows and climbs towards a point known as the Waterhole Slide. The area received its name from the water troughs that early-day freighters kept at this point to give their teams a drink after ascending the steep grades. In the winter, avalanches repeatedly block the road at this point and fill the canyon bottom with enormous amounts of snow that can last all summer. The road is kept open, however, with bulldozers and plows. Through the years, many men and animals have lost their lives in this snowslide which has a catch basin that extends for 2,900 feet above the road.

Three-tenths of a mile past the Waterhole Slide area the main road forks. The right fork leads to the ghost town of Sneffels, the portal of the Revenue Mine and on to Yankee Boy and Governor Basins. The road to the left leads to the private complex of buildings of the Camp Bird Mine. These buildings include a modern mill, the portal of the main haulage tunnel and two Victorian mansions which were once homes for the mine and mill superintendents.

Many stories have been told of the discovery of the Camp Bird Mine. However, a summary of Walsh's own story as he told it to a class of graduating seniors at the Colorado State School of Mines in 1908 should set the record straight. In 1896, Thomas Walsh was operating a small smelter in Silverton. He was looking for ore for use as flux and his prospecting trip for that purpose eventually led him along the old "Highline Trail" that had been established in 1875 and was the route used by the earliest prospectors and miners between Silverton and the Imogene and Sneffels districts. Self taught though he was, Walsh was considerably more knowledgeable in the fields of geology and minerology than was the average prospector. As he was crossing Imogene Basin, he noticed, one lone man puttering around one of the old claims that had previously been worked and abandoned as too low-grade to be profitable. Walsh stopped to chat with him - a man who soon became his fast friend and part-time employee. The man was Andy Richardson who was one of the first to arrive in the area in 1875 and had staked some of the earliest claims. With Andy's aid, Walsh thoroughly prospected most of the basin. On one occasion, while recovering from an illness, he asked Andy to tunnel through snow that covered one of the old adits and get him some samples from the breast of the drift where the former operation had ended. Before he was completely well, Walsh rode his horse up to the cabin being used by Andy (Walsh was now living in Ouray). He found that Andy had brought out several sacks of the vein rock that the former operators had considered the only thing of value in the mine. Walsh decided, over Andy's protestations (for Walsh was not yet fully recovered), to go in and get his own samples. He became interested in the rock that lay alongside the shiny, showy vein. His experience and knowledge of minerals told him it might well contain gold. When samples from diggings on the Una and Gertrude claims were assayed, they showed gold ore worth $3,000 per ton. Quietly, Walsh set about buying the two claims for $10,000.00 and eventually owned nearly all the other claims in the basin. When he returned home to Ouray, he whispered to his daughter Evalyn: "Daughter, I've struck it rich!" The mine's name supposedly came from the jays that stole crumbs from the Walshes when they first picnicked on the spot.

Between 1896 and 1910, the mine produced over twenty-six million dollars. Evalyn told of "the great gold engine" which roared twenty-four hours a day and each day left her father $5,000.00 richer. In its early years the mine's net profits were at the highest rate ever achieved by any mine in Colorado's history. It was world famous!

Almost simultaneously with the opening of the mine, Walsh began building his mill, located at the confluence of Sneffels and Imogene creeks, two miles below the mine in Imogene basin. All the ore was transported from mine to mill by means of a two-mile long aerial tramway, which system remained in use for sometime after the mine was

The Camp Bird milling complex. At extreme left is the cyanide mill, just left of center the huge stamp mill and center foreground is the office, dwellings, boardinghouse, two dormitories and the "gold room"—the place where the gold concentrate from the mill was amalgamated, retorted and made into ingots for shipment to the U.S. Mint in Denver. This picture was made during the years after the mine was sold to Camp Bird Limited of London. Until 1916, ore was delivered to the mill by means of a two-mile-long aerial tramway from the mine in Imogene Basin. Mining ceased in that year and the effort was in the drilling of an 11,000-foot tunnel, beginning at the level of the mill and extending beneath the old workings. Water could now be drained from all the old shafts, eliminating the cost of pumping, and ore could be trammed directly to the mill by train, thus doing away with the old aerial tram. (Colorado Historical Society)

sold to an English syndicate, the Camp Bird Limited. The mill, the assay plant, the amalgamating or "gold room" and Walsh's office were all located at the lower site. The large Victorian houses, however, were not built there until after the mine had been sold by Walsh in 1902 to the English syndicate for a price in excess of $5,000,000. Walsh did have a two-level cabin at the mine site for his own use whenever he stayed there. It stood until about 1957 when vandals (part-time employees who had been assigned to do some work there) found a case of dynamite,

Camp Bird Mill complex as viewed from the down-creek side. At lower left, the Camp Bird School, the second school building at Camp Bird. The first school was destroyed by an avalanche, fortunately at night when there were no occupants. Since that time the avalanche that sometimes runs at that location has been called the "Schoolhouse Slide." The new school, needless to say, was built in a different location and survived for many years. (Denver Public Library)

placed the explosives in the cabin and blew it up. The larger of the two big houses at the mill site was built for the general manager. As long as Camp Bird Limited operated the mine, the manager was always from England and always single! After the sale, Walsh built a large mansion in Washington D.C. where the family entertained lavishly. Evalyn, who married Ned McLean, heir to a newspaper publishing fortune, became known for her expensive parties and acquisition of jewels, including the Hope Diamond. She became the friend of the rich and politically affluent and her parties became the talk of the nation's capital.

Under the auspices of Camp Bird Limited, which purchased the mine from Tom Walsh, the Camp Bird continued production until 1916 when work was halted to drive an 11,000-foot haulage tunnel which also served to drain water from the lower levels. The mine and mill have been worked off and on since that time. The present mill was built in 1960 and can treat five hundred tons of ore a day from the Camp Bird and other mines in the region.

The area is much the same today as in 1903 when Robert Livermore, in **Bostonians and Bullion**, described it as:

"one of real grandeur and beauty, an amphitheater of towering cliffs, with their toes covered with slide rock, surrounded slopes thickly carpeted with grass and flowers in the short summer, deep buried in snow eight months of the year. Tall spruce forests still covered the lower slopes and in the distance, where the valley opened a vista, the vertical-sided top of Potosi towered against the sky line...Up above us there were little flats, glacial cirques, real mountain meadows, usually with a small lake in the center, simply ablaze with flowers, the beautiful columbine, painter's brush, and many alpine varieties unknown to me. Sometimes in one of these, out of sight of the transit man below, I would lie on the mossy sward, smoke a pipe, hear the bees humming, the sweet call of the white-crowned sparrow, and watch the cottony clouds go by in the sparkling blue air, for the moment my own master."

At a spot known as the "drinking cup" on the Sneffels Road. The culvert carries water beneath the road from the springs that gush out of the cliff at the right. During the days when great trains of ore wagons (each pulled by six husky horses) were daily plying the road, tin cups were kept hanging near the springs so that the wagon drivers could get a cold drink of delicious spring water to clear the dust from their throats—hence the name "drinking cup." Here, too, is a spectacular overlook down into deep Canyon Creek Gorge. (Bill Fries III)

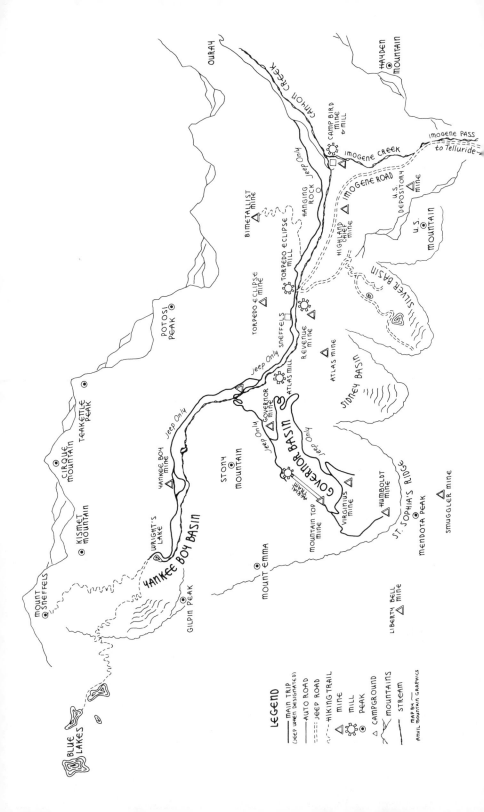

CHAPTER 9
Yankee Boy and Governor Basin
Half-way to Heaven

The high tundra of Yankee Boy and Governor basins may be only half-way to heaven, but in mid-summer, when their meadows are carpeted with Alpine wildflowers, the visitor truly feels he has reached paradise. Few areas on earth have a more spectacular backdrop of mountain scenery for a brief but gorgeous summer show of hundreds of varieties of colorful blossoms, dominated by Colorado's state flower, the Blue Columbine.

The roads to both basins are dead ends and beyond the Ruby Trust are for four-wheel-drive vehicles only, not only because compound gearing is required to climb the grades, but also because slow speeds and high clearance are required to negotiate the rough roads. The character of the surfaces can change with the spring runoffs and summer cloudbursts that damage the roadbeds.

Just short of the Camp Bird Mill, a right hand fork in the road begins the journey. Drivers should be continuously alert for trucks as well as four-wheel-drive vehicles on the sometimes narrow shelf road. At the first major bend in the road a spectacular view of the Camp Bird complex can be seen directly below. Also, at this bend and directly beside the road is the Jackpot Mine which has had off-and-on operations.

Just beyond this point, the road passes under Hanging Rock, obviously named because the cliffs actually hang over the right-of-way cut out of solid rock. In the next few miles, the ruins of old mines (the most visible being the Highland Chief) can be glimpsed across the gorge of Sneffels Creek. Tributary waterfalls gush down the canyon wall. A short distance past this stretch, a road branches to the right; now impassible for vehicles, but can be hiked to the Bimetalist Mine. The mine was located in the 1890s by Malcolm Downer, a miner at the Revenue who prospected in his spare time. For a few years it produced very profitable amounts of silver and lead.

Shortly past the Bimetalist cutoff, the road turning off to the left is well marked as going to Imogene Pass and to Telluride. (See Chapter 10). To the right is Potosi Peak, 13,790 feet. On the same side of the road and shortly above the Imogene turnoff is Torpedo Eclipse Mine. The "mill" at the site of the Torpedo Eclipse is actually the old commissary. A promotor from Tennessee in the 1950s installed some milling equipment in the old building with the purpose of milling ore from both the Torpedo-Eclipse and the Ruby Trust located further up the valley. Before that time the mine was connected to the Revenue Mill across the creek by an aerial tram.

Just a short distance further, the road passes through the ghost town of Sneffels (also called Mt. Sneffels) named for the tallest mountain in

Mount Sneffels (the town) with Stony Mountain in background. At far right can be seen Porter's store and the post office, then next left, a dwelling house and beyond that, another. In foreground, at left, are mule barns. The mule barns were standing until 1951 when an avalanche, that had never run before, to anyone's memory, roared down from Mt. Potosi and swept them away. (Ruth Gregory Collection)

These miners are not just posing, they're "showing off" with their drinks in front of the early Mt. Sneffels Post Office. (Ruth Gregory Collection)

the district by the Hayden Survey Party. "Sneffels is a spelling variation of the Icelandic Mt. Snaefel in Jules Verne's book 'A Journey to the Center of the Earth.' " Sneffels (the mountain) cannot be seen from Sneffels (the town) or vice versa. The remains of the settlement include the well maintained Revenue Mine buildings as well as several small houses, commercial buildings and sheds. The first cabin built in the area was built in 1875 when Quinn and Richardson came over from the Silverton area. Many rich mines were subsequently discovered nearby. But dominating the area was the Revenue-Virginius Mill and Tunnel which produced gold and silver ore worth over $27 million between 1876 and the late 1940s. At its peak the mill and mine are reputed to have employed more than 400 men.

A freight wagon and a burrow train in front of Porter's store. In the background, at center, the Revenue Mill. The long, low structure extending from the top of the mill to the right margin of picture is the "snow tunnel," leading from the mine portal to the mill. All the buildings in upper right are part of the Revenue complex. (Denver Public Library)

Bird's-eye view of the Revenue Mine complex. Full length of the snow tunnel, described in the previous caption, may be seen here. (Colorado Historical Society)

The famous Virginius Mine, 1,000 feet above timberline. Located in 1875, the mine was a fabulous producer. After shafts became very deep, hoisting ore and pumping water became very expensive. The Revenue Tunnel was bored, primarily to tap into the Virginius workings from below, thus eliminating altogether hoisting and pumping problems. (Denver Public Library)

At home in Mount Sneffels. (Ruth Gregory Collection)

The small village of Sneffels (called Porters originally) contained a post office and a general store operated by a Colonel Porter who was also a commercial photographer of some repute. The daily hauling of some 40 tons of mill concentrates from the Revenue Tunnel to Ouray required a large stable of draft horses owned by John Ashenfelter. The 1890 census showed 90 inhabitants in the Porter area and 270 in the Mt. Sneffels precinct. By 1900, the census listed 442 plus 9 at the Virginius. The population then declined to only 144 persons in 1920 and a mere 21 in 1930.

The Virginius Mine was started far above Sneffels in 1876 at an elevation of 12,500 feet in Humboldt Basin, sometimes called Virginius Basin. A small settlement including a post office grew up around the mine. The fabulously rich silver vein was followed down by shaft and crosscut tunnels until ultimately it reached 1,670 feet below the surface. The hardships of winter operation, the difficulties of hauling ore and the problems of pumping water from the shaft led to the driving of the Revenue Tunnel for a distance of 7,800 feet. It was completed in 1893 to intersect the lower Virginius workings some 2,900 feet below the surface.

Prime mover in development of the Revenue-Virginius was Albert E. Reynolds who joined forces with the Thatcher brothers to purchase the property and develop large-scale production. Operations continued year 'round despite the constant winter hazard of avalanches. The $600,000 cost of the tunnel was more than paid for by ore encountered enroute through the mountain. The mine was Colorado's first to light its interior and power its ore cars by electricity. However, there were no switches and cans were put over the bulbs in the boardinghouse at night. Power was generated by hydroelectric plants. Eventually, there were three of these generating stations along the creeks and a huge coal-fired generating plant was built at Ouray. Although alternating current was coming into use, it still hadn't gained superiority over direct current. For whatever reasons, the Revenue's owner - the Caroline Mining Company - built all these generating plants to supply direct current, which soon proved too costly to transmit over the eight-mile lines. It was found that money could actually be saved in buying power from the Telluride Power Co. and the mining company's own plants were closed down.

Just beyond the Revenue, and still in the area of Sneffels town, are the decaying remains of the Atlas Mill, tumbling down the mountainside. Until 1950, a large three-story bunk and boardinghouse stood in the flat just below the mill. It was torn down, moved to Ouray and most of the material used in the framing of the Antlers Motel. The Atlas Mill is still connected to the mine by a crumbling aerial tramway extending half a mile up the mountain. Its gold and silver production lasted from the 1890s until the 1920s when it closed. The mill was very unique for its time. The Colorado Bureau of Mines wrote a detailed account of its process in 1914. The Mining Journal, in the mid-twenties, featured on its cover a very pretty shot of the Atlas Mill with Stony Mountain (a stark volcanic "stack" which is 12,698 feet at its summit) in the background.

A short distance beyond the Atlas, the right fork in the road leads to Yankee Boy Basin. The left branch leads to Governor Basin and is dealt with later in this chapter. The road to Yankee Boy is usually extremely rough due to washouts caused by the heavy spring snow runoff. Part way up the Basin, the road passes close to Twin Falls, a familiar scene in Coors beer commercials. From this point on, flowers cover the landscape

The Atlas Mill, about a half-mile above the Revenue on Sneffels Creek. The Atlas Mine is high on Mendota Mountain, above the Revenue Tunnel. Ore was delivered to the mill by aerial tramway. The Atlas Mine and Mill were yet in full operation in 1927. The three-story boardinghouse, bottom center, was framed entirely with Oregon fir. Material from this building supplied most of the framing for the Antlers Motel in Ouray. (Denver Public Library)

from the time the snow melts (usually June) until late August, with the peak period being in July. Thousands of blue and white columbine along with purple king's crown, blue chiming bells, deep red Indian paintbrush, and hundreds of other varieties of Alpine blossoms cover the meadows. Visitors are cautioned not to pick the flowers. The forest service admonishes "Take nothing but pictures. Leave nothing but footprints."

Yankee Boy Basin was created by ancient glaciers about 10,000 years ago. Two roads now run through it. The one on the right (high side) is the rougher, but less muddy. The lower road travels through the middle of the basin. Where the roads tie back together is the site of the Yankee Boy Mine. The mine was originally staked by William Weston (a British metallurgist) and George Barber in 1877. It reportedly produced $50,000 in its first year and in 1878 yielded $56,000 to its lessee, F. B. Beaudry (a record for the area at that time). By 1881, the mine had 800 feet of tunnels and had been sold to a New York syndicate. It produced gray copper, ruby silver and brittle silver. Sorted ore averaged 103 to 396 ounces of silver per ton. The mine was still being worked at the turn of the century.

A short distance beyond the mine the road forks. The left branch dead-ends in the basin. The right fork climbs steadily over clay-type soil which is extremely slippery and hazardous in wet weather. At the end of

Yankee Boy Mine above the town of Sneffels, in a yet higher basin which takes its name from the mine—"Yankee Boy Basin." Nothing but the ore dump remains now to mark the location of this mine. (Denver Public Library)

the road is Wright's Mine and Wright's Lake. Wm. Wright, a Cornish miner from the "Old Country," mined (or at least did his assessment work) at this site for many years. For a few years after his death, his son Arthur, with the aid of Grandson Ed, kept up the assessments, but eventually quit. In 1956, they planted 5,000 baby trout in the lake, but none seem to have survived.

Although the road ends near the lake, two hiking trails continue. One difficult trail leads to a saddle connecting the 14,150-foot summit of Sneffels with a lesser peak known as Kismet. If taking this hike, be sure not to head up the mountains to the right too quickly. Several people have been lost or killed by making this mistake! Stay to the west (straight) across the rock field and then up a clearly defined trail to the right. The hike requires about two to three hours to the top. The other path is Blue Lakes Trail, leading two miles up a ridge to a 13,000-foot divide, then down past the three Blue Lakes to Dallas Creek. Both Blue Lakes and Dallas Creek are good fishing spots. For the technical mountain climber, there is also access to Cirque Peak (13,686 feet), Potosi Peak (13,786 feet), and Teakettle Peak (13,819 feet). Gilpin Peak (13,964 feet) is also at the west end of the glacial cirque. It was named for William Gilpin, first territorial governor of Colorado, who was appointed by Abraham Lincoln in 1861. Detailed instructions for climbing the peaks may be found in "Guide to the Colorado Mountains" by Robert Ormes. Visitors are advised not to attempt to climb these mountains unless they are experienced, have proper equipment and good instructions or a guide. Also, acclimatization to the altitude is essential.

132

Just right and a bit above center, the roof of a mill and a smokestack from a boiler-house may be seen. This is the site of the Ruby Trust Mine, just below Yankee Boy Basin. Every mill that has been built at the Ruby Trust has been on the same site as preceding ones and each one has been destroyed by an avalanche! The mountain peak at top is "Kismet" which, from this point, obscures Mt. Sneffels, (the mountain, not the town) which stands directly beyond. (Denver Public Library)

Returning back to the left fork west of the townsite of Sneffels, the road fords Sneffels Creek a short distance below the Ruby Trust Mine which resumed activity in 1979 after years of being closed. In the 1880s and 90s the Ruby Trust produced some very high grade silver-lead ore with ruby silver (an ore that appears to "bleed" when broken open).   The area never had a post office as Sneffels was close enough to be a supply center. The original cabins and mill had been almost completely destroyed by avalanches and fires. Several new structures were built in 1979 and 1980. Three men died when a snowslide hit the mine's boardinghouse in 1886. Again, in 1903 an avalanche destroyed the boardinghouse and bunkhouse and badly damaged the mill. A small mill was set up on the site about 1947 by Emil Leonardi and his sons. It, too, was destroyed by a snowslide the following winter.

Traveling on, the road leads up and around the base of Stony Mountain where a road forks to the right leading to Governor Basin and the base tramway station for the Mountain Top Mine. At the upper end of the tram line in Humboldt (also called Virginius) Basin, the mine is located at 12,000 feet to the northwest of the Virginius. The Mountain Top produced silver and lead. The main operation of the mine closed in 1929 but it has been reopened several times and efforts to do so are again underway. Because of the snowslide hazard, a 60-ton mill was constructed 900 feet underground. It was said to have been the first such installation in the world, but it failed to operate properly. The mine itself can be reached by following the road up and bearing to the right at every juncture.

Traveling upward, sometimes rather steeply, around several switchbacks hewn from the solid rock of Mendota Mountain to make the wagon road, one may see a less used road to the left that leads over the hump into Sidney Basin. Traveling on westward, we eventually reach a point where the Virginius dumps are visible high up on our left; the Humboldt, high up on the wall of the cirque just beneath St. Sophia's Ridge; and across the basin, the Mountain Top Mine. We may choose either the road to the left which leads up to the site of the Virginius or the one to the right, circling around and across the little creek to the Mountain Top Mine. The Humboldt is not attainable by four-wheel-drive vehicle. The Virginius was located by William B. Freeland on June 28, 1876 and soon became one of the area's foremost producers of silver with more than three miles of tunnels. A dozen men worked two shafts and three levels in 1876. Fifteen men worked through the winter of 1877, living in cabins that were sometimes completely buried by snow. The mine's ownership changed hands three times in as many years until its purchase in 1880 by A. E. Reynolds for $100,000. In 1880, Frank Fossett

A winter view of the Virginius Mine at 12,500 feet. In order that this mine could operate through the winter months, great stores of fuel and food had to be laid in during the summertime. There were times when even the pack mules could not be used for several days. (Ruth Gregory Collection)

The combination boardinghouse, bunkhouse at the Mountain Top Mine. Note the great boulder at the uphill end of the building. The structure was deliberately placed there in the hope that should an avalanche come from above, the big rock would split the snow mass and send it around the building on both sides. Looking almost due east, we see Mt. Potosi at right which is volcanic in origin but is composed of volcanic "tuff" or ash, unlike its near neighbor, Stony Mountain. Stony is "magma" or cooled, hardened, formerly molten lava. (Ruth Gregory Collection)

reported that "the Virginius is as good a mine as there is in this region...It is badly situated for working, being in an almost inaccessible position." Thirteen men were at work at that time. The mine averaged about eight ounces of gold and 175 ounces of silver in its earlier years, but the ore got richer as it went deeper. Eventually, more than 100 miners lived at the three-story boardinghouse located at the upper level of the mine. Several rather ghastly accidents happened at the mine. In 1883, a slide hit the boardinghouse killing four men. If men were not buried in avalanches, they were blown to bits while trying to thaw dynamite or when tamping powder into a hole which still contained an unspent charge. For example, Reverend J. J. Gibbons in his book In the San Juan recites in detail the tragic story of Billy Maher, who constructed a cabin near the Virginius in an area where tundra was the only vegetation and the marmot, chipmunk and ptarmigan the only animals. During the winter his wife stayed in town. One cold day, while thawing eight sticks of dynamite on his stove, the powder went off. Billy's right hand was blown off, his clothes were ripped to shreds and he was deaf and blind. Billy lay near death. Billy's partner set off downhill for help at the Terrible Mine about a mile away. Billy's dog went uphill to the Humboldt but couldn't get any of the miners to follow him back down. It took Billy's partner almost eight hours to make the one-mile trip to the Terrible. Four men set out and found Billy. They constructed a sled and set off. Darkness fell and a storm came up, but the men made it back to the Terrible. The next morning the men from the Terrible called the

St. Sophia's Ridge. In the big cirque beneath the ridge are situated this Mountain Top Mine (faintly seen at lower right), the Humboldt, the Virginius and Terrible mines. (Ruth Gregory Collection)

Virginius to find out why four men from Virginius had not come to the Terrible. They had planned to be there the previous evening. Only then did the men at the Terrible learn the Virginius men had set out. A rescue party found all four dead in an avalanche. One, Allen McIntyre, lived for five or six hours - buried alive before he froze to death (as shown by a space a foot above him melted away by his breath). The other three had been killed instantly. None of the bodies were over four feet under the surface and one of the men's hands were within inches of the surface. Billy Maher died anyway.

Injuries and death from snowslides were frequent, until finally in 1893, completion of the Revenue access tunnel enabled operators to close the upper buildings. While the upper workings were active, the mine had its own post office which according to post cards from the area, was the nation's highest. A small store was also located at the mine.

Above the Virginius, at an altitude of 12,700 feet, is the Humboldt Mine. At one time it employed about 180 men. Shortly before World War I, the best claims were sold to the Smuggler Union Mining Co. whose main adit (opening) was located on the opposite side of St. Sophia Ridge. The purchase came about as a result of litigation. The operators of the Humboldt discovered that the Smuggler had been mining Humboldt ore from underneath their own workings. Humboldt sued to recover the value of the ore mined by the Smuggler and the latter was given the choice of paying an appraised sum for the ore mined or buying the claims (in which case they could continue to mine them). They chose the latter

Burro train, loaded with supplies for the Virginius Mine. Even in the best of weather, such cargo as could be carried by burro was often more conveniently and more economically transported this way than by wagon. Heavy machinery, many tons of coal and very large timbers, of course, required the use of wagons. The wagons used for this must be very sturdily built and pulled by never less than six powerful horses, driven by the world's most skillful drivers. (Ruth Gregory Collection)

course. The Humboldt was also plagued with snowslides, Rev. Gibbons wrote in 1898 that the foreman of the mine was out in a snowstorm so thick that he could not see and fell to his death over a 500-foot cliff.

The jagged pinnacles of St. Sophia Ridge rise behind the Humboldt and Virginius to over 13,000 feet. The ridge is also visible from Telluride and the old trail to Telluride crosses its southern end. The trail forks after crossing the ridge, but both branches go to Telluride, the left fork via

Marshall basin and the right fork via the Liberty Bell Mine and Cornet Creek. The ridge itself is unsafe to climb because of crumbling rock and even on the trail the climb is rough and extremely dangerous. In the late 1800s, the accepted practice for one way of travel between Ouray and Telluride was to ride a horse to the Virginius, then walk across the ridge to the Smuggler Mine where the traveler got another horse to ride to Telluride.

Virginius ore, brought down the mountain as far as Sneffels by burrow and stored under the snowshed, is here reloaded into wagons for the remainder of the trip to Ouray. There, it will again be transferred, this time into railroad cars. The wagon at the left is powered by six, wiry, muscular mules. (Ruth Gregory Collection)

Ruins such as this one are found in many places throughout the San Juan mining region. Visitors should be aware that these properties are still owned, either by mining companies or individuals who continue to pay taxes on them. Removal of lumber, old machinery or other objects found there may be seen as anything from vandalism to grand theft. (Bill Fries III)

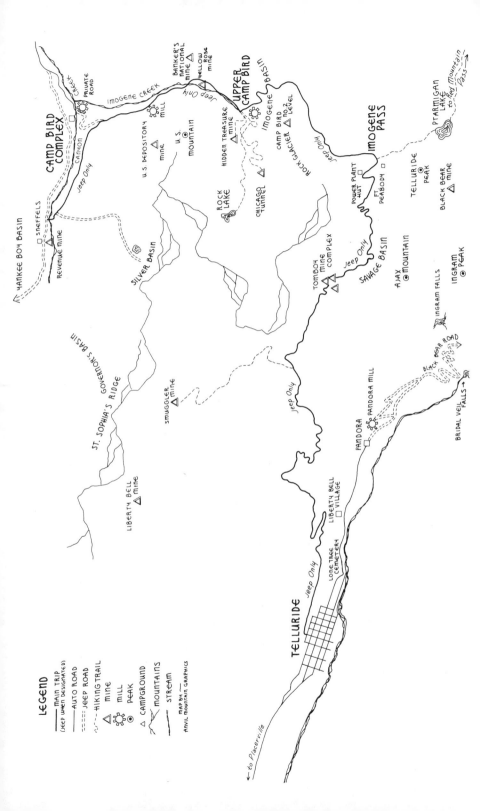

CHAPTER 10
Imogene Pass
The High Road to Telluride

A "shortcut" between Ouray and Telluride, via Imogene Pass, is usually open about six to eight weeks in August and September. However, after winters of exceptional snows, the upper part of the road is closed all summer. The road peaks at 13,114 feet above sea level and is the second highest vehicular pass in North America. It is definitely limited to four-wheel-drive vehicles and is exceeded in height only by 13,180-foot Mosquito Pass between Alma and Leadville, Colorado.

One road to Imogene Pass starts from the Camp Bird headquarters. However, it goes through private lands, and visitors are asked to gain access by taking the turnoff from the Camp Bird-Revenue Road just south of the town of Sneffels. Ford Sneffels Creek and travel for one and one half miles to join the road coming directly up from the Camp Bird. The route is bumpy, sometimes muddy, and crossed by several small streams. It lies atop a cliff near the base of United States Mountain and affords a view directly down on the Camp Bird Mill's buildings and on down Canyon Creek to the mountains beyond Ouray.

Just past the road junction, the traveler will observe the remains of the U.S. Depository Mill which served a mine of the same name located in 1877 by George L. Wright. The mine is higher up U.S. Mountain and was eventually abandoned because it was, unfortunately, built in the path of one of the area's biggest and most frequent snowslides. A sawmill located across the creek furnished lumber and timber for the mine.

Beyond the U.S. Mill the road crosses Imogene Creek (don't try the bridge). A branch to the right immediately before the crossing dead-ends a short distance at the Yellow Rose Mine. The main road crosses the creek and ascends a shelf road. Shortly before the road recrosses Imogene Creek, a branch to the left leads to Richmond Basin and the Bankers National Mine. Several men were killed and most of the buildings of this mine were destroyed by avalanches in 1905. The main road leads to the right to Imogene Basin and the ruins of the Upper Camp Bird Mine.

Imogene Basin was one of the first areas in the Sneffels Mining District to be prospected. Andy Richardson entered from the Silverton area in 1875 and named the mountain basin after his wife. Twenty years later the same Richardson became fast friends with Tom Walsh and aided him in the prospecting of the basin and the discovery of the fabulous Camp Bird Mine. The basin was the site of the first rich discoveries in Ouray County and was occupied year round from 1876 until 1949. Snowslides always made life hazardous.

In the basin to the north was the first really large operation in the area—the Hidden Treasure. It was discovered on October 7, 1875 by

The Camp Bird Mine (upper camp) looking north at about 11,500 feet in Imogene Basin. In the early years of operation, the ore was transported by aerial tramway to the mill, two miles away and 1,500 vertical feet down. Beyond the mine buildings and at center may be seen the three-story boardinghouse, built to accommodate four hundred miners. In 1899, a convention of newspaper publishers and writers from all over Colorado convened at Ouray and were entertained at a banquet here on orders of Tom Walsh. Later, in their papers, most of the writers referred to this boardinghouse as the Camp Bird's "wonderful hotel." (Colorado Historical Society)

When at Camp Bird, Mr. Walsh had his own private quarters. The Walsh cabin, shown here, remained until about 1956 when it was destroyed by vandals. (Ruth Gregory Collection)

W.H. Brookover and Edward Wright who came from Silverton partially by snowshoe. First tests showed hand-picked ore running 1200 ounces of silver to the ton. In 1880, Fossett reported that "a smelter is being erected . . . The ore bodies are usually large and permanent, with galena the base of the metals. The lower workings are said to show better mineral than was found on the surface." It was one of the prominent veins of the Sneffels Mining District. It continued to produce large quantities of ore into the 1920s and 1930s and was retained by Walsh and his family when he sold the Camp Bird Mine to an English mining syndicate. Snowslides and winds have reduced the mine buildings to debris around the tunnel entrance. Higher up in the basin lies the portal of the Chicago Tunnel, cut from solid rock. Higher still in the basin is

Upper Camp Bird, looking south. The big boardinghouse, described in the previous caption, is seen at right. The tower-like structure at extreme left with the little house on top is the tram-house, where the ore buckets began their two-mile, downhill journey to the mill. (Colorado Historical Society)

Rock Lake. Although no trail of consequence leads to it, the surrounding area shows signs of habitation in the form of discarded shoes, tin cans, and old boards. Walsh did not stint on the amenities at the Camp Bird Mine. In the wilderness near the No. 3 level in Imogene Basin, he built a three-story boardinghouse that would accommodate 400 men in a state of steam-heated comfort to which miners were not accustomed. It had hardwood floors, tongue-and-groove wainscotting, bathrooms with hot and cold water, panels of marble, tubs and wash basins of finest porcelain, electric lights and telephones. Recreation rooms and a library were provided. And the bill of fare in the dining rooms was, in contrast to the usual "sowbelly and beans," the best food obtainable in the region. A tradition at Camp Bird was that any traveler passing through the basin could be assured of an excellent meal at no charge.

But Imogene Basin was cold and the snow piled deep in the winter. The miners told tales that when a man whistled, his notes would freeze and when they all thawed out in the spring, the woods sounded like a steam calliope. The snow became so deep that packers would place rags in the tops of trees to blaze trails. In the summer, tourists were told that the birds put them there to find their way home on cold snowy nights!

Avalanches posed a constant threat in Imogene as in other high basins and a double chevron defense built about 1900 is still visible on the talus slope above Camp Bird's No. 2 level portal. In 1897, a slide buried three of the miners in their cabin but they escaped unhurt. In April 1900, one man was killed and one was injured. Again in March 1902, a slide killed one man and injured four. In 1906, two snowslides demolished the mill two and one half miles down-valley from the mine and badly damaged the bunkhouse. Six men were injured and one was killed. On February 24, 1936, Rose Israel (camp cook), Chapp Woods (mill superintendent)

Residents of Camp Bird's "hotel" posing on the steps that lead up to the entrances. These men are dressed in their "off-shift" clothes or in their "goin-to-town" clothes. (Ruth Gregory Collection)

On top of Imogene Pass, 13,385 feet above sea level. The building in the picture is the hut where the service and maintenance man watched over the lines of the Telluride Power Co., which were strung over the pass to serve Camp Bird and the mines in the Sneffels district. At first, the mines used the power chiefly for lights. They were billed, not for kilowatts used, but at a price per light, per month. (Bill Fries III)

and Ralph Klinger (camp blacksmith) were killed and the mill, bunkhouse and other buildings of the Upper Camp Bird were badly damaged when three or four slides all ran simultaneously. However, the next morning rebuilding had already begun.

Proceeding on our trip upward, the road slants across steep talus slopes to reach the final approaches to Imogene Pass. In early years, electric power for the Camp Bird came across the pass from the plant at Ames (near Telluride) which generated the first commercially-sold alternating current in the world. The lines across the pass were the highest in North America and a company repairman was stationed in the corrugated metal hut (which still stands atop the pass) warmed against the sub-zero winter temperatures by electric heaters. Only a trail led up the east side of the pass until 1966 when San Miguel and Ouray counties split the cost of a road.

From the top, Ptarmigan Lake is visible to the south as well as all three Red Mountains. At one time the lake was the only source of water for the mines in Savage Basin located below the west side of the pass. A man was kept there at all times to keep the pumps operating. From the top of the pass, pack trails lead down the Highline Trail to the Red Mountain area. Visible above the road a short distance south of the pass is "Fort Peabody." A pile of stones—actually a large rock cairn which supported a flagpole—was still standing and a flag was flying from it when the jeep road was opened in 1968. Also, a small shelter hut was built during the labor troubles in 1904 when a squad of militia was stationed there to prevent deported troublemakers from returning to Telluride over the pass. Since the state militia moved only on order from the governor, it was Governor Peabody who had sent the militia to Telluride. "Peabody's Fort" is actually a sarcasm first applied by the striking miners. The top of the pass also affords a view of much of the San Juan Mountains, the La Sal Mountains to the northwest in Utah and the Sneffels Range to the north.

The road going down seven miles through Savage Basin to Telluride is an easier grade than on the Ouray side. Savage Basin is a glacial cirque in which the road levels out at about 11,500 feet. Scattered everywhere are the ruins of what was the Tomboy camp. The valley was once filled with mine buildings, a large 60 stamp mill, livery stables, a school, homes, machine shops, a store, a three-story boardinghouse for 250 men and even a bowling alley. The Tomboy was discovered in 1880. In 1897, the property was sold to the Rothschilds of London for $2 million. Winter life in Savage Basin is vividly described in Harriet Backus' "Tomboy Bride." It was a never-ending battle against cold, deep snow, and avalanches. She reported that snowdrifts built up to twenty feet and avalanches boomed down the slopes. All supplies were delivered by mule, which then took the concentrates from the mill down to Telluride. Poor Mrs. Backus even found her silverware arranged on the floor by the pack rats! The Tomboy closed in 1927 and most buildings were razed for scrap during World War II. Work underground was resumed, however, with the consolidation of the Tomboy and several other mines in the area under the auspices of the Idarado Mining Co.

Over a ridge to the northwest, and adjacent to Savage Basin, is Marshall Basin which contains the Smuggler Mine, attainable only by trail. It was so named because it was located in a missurveyed area between the Sheridan and the Union claims, both discovered in 1874. In 1900, the claims were consolidated and soon became one of the largest workings in Colorado with 35 miles of tunnels. One of the gold veins was over a mile long. Eventually a tram line was built to Pandora, east of Telluride, where a mill was constructed. In its peak years, the mine employed 900 men. Although the mine produced millions in extremely rich ore, it paid no great profits due to huge operating costs and the fact it normally could be operated for only six or seven months a year. It ceased operations under its own management in 1928, but eventually was continued under Telluride Mines and Idarado.

Not far from the Smuggler, and several miles before Telluride, is the Liberty Bell Mine discovered in 1876 by W.L. Cornett. It was not greatly productive until 1897 when a rich vein was discovered. By 1917, over $16 million had been taken from the mine and a mill was constructed at Liberty Bell Village, about midway between Telluride and Pandora. Again showslides were a danger. In 1902, successive snowslides killed 19. The mine closed in 1921.

The main road continues on a zigzag downward route, going through a short tunnel, and eventually reaching Telluride on the floor of the valley of the San Miguel River. Before reaching town, a spectacular view unfolds: Bridal Veil Falls, the switchbacks of the Black Bear Road and Ingram Falls on the east headwall of the valley.

The area around Telluride was first settled about 1875. In 1876, about one hundred persons lived in the area. At first, San Miguel City, which had an earlier start two miles to the west, was larger than Telluride (named Columbia at the time), but the latter town grew and outdistanced San Miguel because of its closer proximity to the area's mines.

Tomboy Camp, Mine and Mill in Savage Basin, on the Telluride side of Imogene Pass. Tomboy is just at timberline, almost the identical elevation of Camp Bird, just over the pass. This was one of the great gold mines in the region and owned, for most of its years of operation, by English investors. Operations here ceased about 1927, but the mine has been worked in recent times through the maze of interconnected tunnels of the Idarado mines. (Colorado Historical Society)

The town of Columbia was incorporated September 30, 1879, but later in 1887 changed its name to Telluride. Many writers make much of Telluride's being named for Tellurium. In fact, tellurium ore has been found in only a few, small, isolated pockets. The postal department objected to "Columbia" because of having another city in California with the same name, and because so many people would abbreviate Col. and Cal. indistinguishably. Crofutt reported in 1885 that Columbia contained "one bank, stores of all kinds, several hotels, one 20 and one 40 stamp mill, one weekly newspaper - The News - and a population of about 1400." He especially touted the placer mining along the San Miguel River. In 1890, the Sheridan Hotel was built, while the opera house next door was added in 1914. The Opera House seats 200 and is connected to the hotel by a second story walkway.

In 1898 Rev. J.J. Gibbons wrote that:

"Telluride is a typical mountain town, progressive and having an enterprising population. Many of the modern improvements are found there, and its pretty residences are set off by the graceful trees which grow along the streets. At some distance may be seen the snowcapped peaks of

This birds-eye view of Telluride is from the one-lane, winding, twisting wagon (jeep) road from the Tomboy Mine to the town of Telluride. (Colorado Historical Society)

Marshall Basin which contain the great mines which have given Telluride a prosperous community."

In November 1890, the Rio Grande Southern Railroad reached the town and stimulated the economic growth. The population approached 5,000, but prosperity was interrupted by the Silver Crash of 1893. However, five years later major gold deposits were discovered and Telluride roared right back to a population of 3,000 at the zenith of the gold boom.

At the turn of the century, Telluride not only could have been, but was the prototype for Wild West movies of later years. It had all the ingredients of a wild and wooly frontier mining town. It supported 26 brothels or "parlor houses," saloons enough to match the number of houses in the red light district and over 175 women employed by the madams, including some with names like "Diamond Tooth Leona" and "Jew Fanny." The San Miguel Valley Bank was once robbed by Butch Cassidy's gang. Jim Clark, a one-time member of Jesse James' gang, served as a deputy marshall and at the same time reportedly broke the law repeatedly while out of town. The Lone Tree Cemetery contains the graves of many outlaws.

Labor troubles between miners and management of the mines contributed to the unrest of the period. In 1901, about 250 miners armed with rifles, shotguns and revolvers stationed themselves behind rocks and trees around the Smuggler Union property where non-union miners were working. When the latter refused to quit work, both sides opened fire and, after several hours of shooting, the non-union force surrendered with casualties amounting to three dead and six seriously wounded. The non-union men were ordered to leave Telluride.

A year later, Arthur Collins, manager of the Smuggler-Union, was shot dead as he sat chatting with friends in the manager's residence in Pandora. Bulkeley Wells succeeded him as manager. In September 1903, the men at Telluride's mills struck for reduction of hours from 12 to 8 hours per day. The next month, 100 miners at the Tomboy walked out in sympathy. Colorado National Guard troops arrived in November and non-union workers were brought in to replace the strikers. Bulkeley Wells served as a Captain commanding Troop A, First Squadron Cavalry. Union workers who caused trouble were deported and martial law was declared in the district. Unrest and disturbances continued many months into 1904, culminating in an unsuccessful bombing attempt that did not harm, but blew Bulkeley Wells out of his house.

In its early days, Telluride boasted that it was the best lighted town in the world with some of the world's first alternating current being used from the nearby Ames generating plant. The plant was designed by George Westinghouse and originally ramrodded by L.L. Nunn so he could supply power to the Gold King Mine. There was also a power plant on the top of Bridal Veils Falls. However, the power plant did not get any energy from Bridal Veil Falls itself for it sits on top of them. A pipeline extended far up Bridal Veil Creek to a lake and delivered water under high pressure to a Pelton Wheel. This was not a commercial plant but was wholly owned by the Smuggler Union (later Telluride Mines Inc.) and supplied power for their mines and mill. When Idarado acquired Telluride Mines Inc., the still-operating power plant was part of the package. Its output, however, was inadequate for all of Idarado's needs and it was closed down.

One of Telluride's larger-than-life legends concerns a swindle perpetrated during the crash of 1929. Charles D. Waggoner, president of the Bank of Telluride, pulled off a $500,000 fraud on banks of New York in order to protect the savings of his own depositors when he realized the bank would soon be closed by examiners. The ruse was short-lived. At the trial, his attorney characterized him as a Robin Hood who stole from the rich to protect his poor depositors, but in spite of this novel defense, Waggoner was convicted.

Metal markets in the 1920s, however, became so depressed that most of Telluride's big mines were compelled to close down—but the town refused to die! (Miners must be resourceful folk in order to live, mining being the erratic business that it is). Telluride was blessed with a goodly supply of enterprising people who found a way to survive, keeping their city alive, providing income for many citizens and some to actually thrive! A manufacturing industry was the answer. Although raw materials could be brought in by the Rio Grande Southern, the distribution of the product could not be by the same means. But if the product could not be delivered to the market, the market would come get it! That product gained a fine reputation for its quality, earned glory for the town, and provided a living for many of its citizens. However, just as it was an act of Congress in 1893 (repeal of the Sherman Silver Purchase Act) that spelled doom for Telluride's silver mining industry; so it was, another act of Congress in 1933 (the repeal of the 18th Amendment—"Prohibition") that effectively put Telluride out of the manufacturing business.

At about that time, mining began a revival that would, in large part, bring Telluride back to good economic health until the late 1970s when metal markets again would no longer support the mining industry.

Again, a new enterprise came along just in time to "save" Telluride: a recreation industry based on snow and scenery. Not only have the giant ski runs with their chair lifts attracted many sports-minded people to the city in the winter, but in the summer months, among other things, the city hosts a "Blue Grass" music festival, a jazz festival and an international hang-glider competition. Telluride is fast becoming a cultural mecca in the San Juan region of Colorado.

East of Telluride is the small town of Pandora, currently the site of the Idarado Mill, formerly the Smuggler-Union Mill. Another mill located here in earlier days was the Pandora Gold Mining Company Mill (a smaller mill of the Smuggler-Union). A tramway terminal of the Tomboy Gold Mine was also in the area so that the concentrates from their mill in Savage Basin could be unloaded for shipment by rail. A large tailings pond now surrounds the area at the western portal of the Idarado Mine — a consolidation of most of the old mines in the area. In spite of the fact Pandora was subject to frequent snowslides over the years, it had 100 inhabitants in 1902.

Four-wheel-drive roads from the Telluride area, aside from the Imogene Pass route, include the switchbacks of the Black Bear Road coming down Ingram Mountain to the east, the Ophir Pass Road starting from Ophir Junction south of Telluride on Highway 145, and the Last Dollar Road which takes off to the northwest from Society Turn three miles west of Telluride. The Ophir Road comes out on U.S. 550 near Burro Bridge between Red Mountain Pass and Silverton. The Last Dollar Road can be traversed for some distance by conventional autos, but is rough in places and should not be attempted at all in wet weather as it has stretches of side hill clay. It comes out on Highway 62 just west of the

The Idarado Mill at Pandora (formerly the Smuggler Mill). From the mill-level portal it is possible to travel through the mountains and emerge from the Treasury Tunnel portal in the Red Mountain district, though the route is quite devious—left, right, straight ahead, up a thousand feet, down a few hundred feet, then up some more and down some more. (Bill Fries III)

crest of Dallas Divide. Black Bear Road starts at the top of Red Mountain Pass on U.S. 550. It is one-way going west, down to Telluride.

Bridal Veil Falls, above Pandora Mill east of Telluride. Atop this vertical cliff, at the top of the falls, is a hydroelectric power plant, formerly used to supply power for the mill at Pandora and the Smuggler Mine in Marshall Basin. No power was sold commercially, but was used solely by Telluride Mines, Inc. After the Smuggler Mine and Mill became part of the Idarado complex, the output of the power plant was insufficient for the needs of Idarado mines and the plant was closed down and power purchased from a commercial supplier. (Bill Fries III)

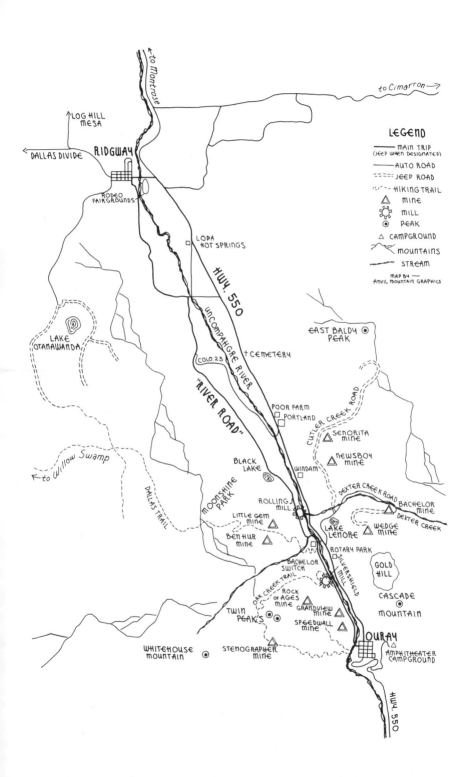

CHAPTER 11
Ouray to Ridgway
You're in Hot Water

This trip consists of traveling down the Uncompahgre River Valley on one side of the river and back on the other. When making the trip remember that most of the mines and sights on one side of the river may be even more visible while traveling the road on the other side. The entire trip can be made by automobile and should take less than half a day.

The origin of the name Uncompahgre is uncertain. Sabin, writing his pamphlet for the **D & RG's Circle Route** reported that "Uncompahgre (un-com-pah-greh) means "red stream" in the Ute language, while early Spaniards called it Rio de San Francisco. But much earlier, Escalante reported "the Utes called it 'Ancapagari' which the interpreter tells us means Colorado Lake from the fact that near its source there is a spring of reddish water, hot and disagreeable to the taste." Sgt. Beckwith with Gunnison's party reported it was a combination of Mapunca (hot) with pah (springs). Carhart reported that it meant "high mountains" in Ute. Another source reported "unca" as "hot," "pah" as "water" and "gre" as "spring." Reader, take your choice; red, standing water is ours. But please, try to pronounce "pah-gree" (rhymes with tree). The word has nothing to do with the Spanish "padre."

There is evidence that the whole area between Ridgway and Ouray is honeycombed with caverns. In early times the area was swampy. Hot water springs appear in both Ouray and Ridgway. All of the springs rose dramatically in 1878 when the area was hit with what appeared to be an earthquake. One theory at that time was that instead of an earthquake, gas had accumulated from the vapor of the hot springs; however, this theory has to be discounted since the tremors were felt as far as ten miles away.

In the early days of Ouray County, a toll road ran from the present site of Colona to Ouray. The toll gate at the Ouray end was near Skyrocket Creek, about midway between the swimming pool and the present Red Mountain Lodge. A fence ran from the river to the cliffs to funnel traffic through the gate at a bridge over the creek.

The Denver & Rio Grande Railroad was built into Ouray in 1887 on the west side of the river and the first train arrived in Ouray on December 15, 1887. This, of course, became Ouray's "lifeline." For many years Ouray had daily freight and passenger service. However, in September of 1930, this became a "mixed train" carrying both passengers and freight. Then in July 1936, only three-day-a-week service; and in March 1953, the equipment was taken away and the rails removed between Ridgway and Ouray. In 1977, the rails were removed between Ridgway and Montrose. Basically the return trip in this chapter on the west side of the Uncompahgre River follows the old railroad line from Ouray.

Engine No. 266 crossing the bridge over the Uncompahgre River at the south end of the city. Just over the tender may be seen the smokestack at the Ouray Power and Light plant. The plant was equipped to use steam during low water periods when the Pelton wheel could not be used. Across the bridge, tracks served the Rice Lumber Co., the Beaumont Sampler, the foundry and the Revenue power (D.C.) plant. (Ruth Gregory Collection)

At the west end of 7th Avenue in Ouray, trainmen line up for a picture. The man fourth from left is identified as Superintendent of the Railway, W.D. Lee. No date for this photo is available, but if you're a student of ladies' fashions, perhaps the hats worn by the two ladies on the rear platform and the one posing in the car window will help in estimating the date. We would guess before World War I. (Ouray County Historical Society)

Windham, three miles north of Ouray. Here, the first smelter, the Ouray-Norfolk, was built and a small community grew up around it. The writing on this 1886 photo reads "Sampling Works and Fruit Farm of R.H. Higgins." Windham had a post office from Dec. 9, 1878 to June 20, 1881. Now, no trace of Windham remains except for six crabapple trees which, as last we knew, were still producing fruit. A small ore-mill now occupies part of what was the fruit farm. (Denver Public Library)

Going north on Highway 550 out of the City limits of Ouray, one passes Rotary Park on the east. There is no camping on the spot, but picnic tables and restrooms are available. The park used to be a large animal cemetery for Ouray (called the "Horse Cemetery") and every year someone finds some "prehistoric" remains. The site was a thicket of trees and brush when purchased by the Rotary Club (now disbanded) for the City of Ouray. In 1941, the Forest Service and Rotary Club cleared the site and installed the present facilities.

A short distance further, the Dexter Creek Road leaves to the right (See Chapter 13). About a half mile north is Tuffy's corner - named after Tuffy Flor, the undertaker in Ouray for many years. It is a very dangerous corner and as recently as 1975 people have died at the spot when they failed to make the turn at high speeds. In the mid 1950s, Tuffy's corner was improved by blasting the rock-cliff back several feet, making the turn less "tight" and improving visibility. It became known as Tuffy's corner because it occasionally provided a case for the mortuary.

After crossing Dexter Creek bridge, a mill is located to the west of the road . . . The "Roland J." Mill (later called Bay City Mill), named for a young man by the name of Roland Jahnke, was built in recent years to treat Pony Express and Syracuse ore.   Another half mile north is a flat area to the right of the road. This is now private property but the general

155

area used to be the site of Windham, described by George Crofutt in 1885 as a small ranch and post office with a few buildings. It was also the site of the Windham smelter which produced for a short time. All evidences of the mill are now gone.

Half a mile further on is the townsite of Portland (elevation 7,233 feet). According to Jocknick, the town was founded in 1877. The post office was established January 11, 1878. It was situated at the southern tip of Uncompahgre Park, where the Uncompahgre Valley widens enough that some farming could be done. The founders saw a potential for growing and marketing vegetables and other produce to the businesses in Ouray and the many mines in the area. In the beginning, Portland was just a few miles south of the boundary of the Ute reservation. The reservation boundary line was later moved four miles farther north. Although in existence for eight years prior, the town was incorporated March 16, 1886.

Portland narrowly escaped being swallowed up by a larger town in a scheme hatched by Dave Day, publisher of Ouray's "Solid Muldoon," and eight other men. They were listed as the board of directors for "Ramona Town Company" which filed Articles of Incorporation December 18, 1886. The directors included some very powerful and important people such as Otto Mears and David Moffat, president of the D&RG Railroad. Day and Moffat had become friends and they verbally agreed that the new town would become the terminus of the railroad which was then building toward Ouray. In his December 3 issue, Day wrote:

> "Ramona, the terminus (of the railroad) is four miles north of Ouray and the townsite embraces the ranches formerly owned by Jocknick, Brounyard, O'Neal and Plumer as well as those now owned in part by Paquin, Haney, Hosner and

Portland, established in 1877, flourished for ten years as a supplier of fresh farm produce for the town of Ouray and the surrounding mines. It was also a supply center for the Paquin mining district. Being on the main stage line between Ouray and Montrose, Portland maintained its position of importance until the coming of the D&RG railway. The railroad built its tracks up over a high plateau, a couple of miles to the west of Portland, effectively isolating the town from commerce. Pictures of Portland seem to be rare, this being the only one we have been able to find. (Colorado Historical Society)

Hotchkiss. The site chosen for what is to become the metropolis of the San Juan Country is, in point of natural advantages, fertility, convenience to the mines, altitude and grandeur of surroundings, unequalled in any country . . . The idea of a rich and prosperous mining camp at an altitude that permits lawns, fruit, flowers, vegetables, berries and cerials [sic] of most every description, seems almost beyond belief, but such will be Ramona."

The proposed town had several suggested names; first, Dayton, (a contraction of "Day's Town" to memorialize David F. Day, the proponent and chief promoter of the scheme), then Helena, after the wife of David Moffat, then Ramona and finally Chipeta in honor of the wife of Chief Ouray. None of these names, however, were ever recognized by the U.S. Postal Department for there was already an established post office in Portland, an incorporated town which, although it was to have been absorbed by the new and larger town of Chipeta, never lost its corporate identity.

On July 19, 1887, the survey work for the new "Metropolis of the San Juan" was completed and lots went on sale. There was a scramble for lots and some of the new owners immediately set about building. In the first three days thirty businessmen bought lots. The frenzy was of short duration, however, for just seven days later, on July 26, an agreement was reached between the D&RG and the business and mining interests in the Town of Ouray whereby, if Ouray would furnish the right-of-way, grade the roadbed, furnish land for the depot and switchyards (a package worth about $50,000) the railroad would extend the line into Ouray, bypassing Portland (or Chipeta, as it would have become). Of course, the success of the Chipeta scheme was dependent upon the railroad terminating there. David Day was furious when events had taken this turn, for, not only did he fail to reach his "pot of gold," but his "rainbow" faded out as well. To add to his woes, Ouray businessmen withdrew all their advertising from Day's "Solid Muldoon," convinced that Day had tried to "sell out" Ouray.

David Day and George Jackson had acquired large blocks of land in the newly acquired portion of the townsite of Chipeta and each had built on his holdings even before the completion of the survey and offering for sale of town lots. Day built a home and a building to house his Solid Muldoon and printing establishment (the home remained in the Day family and was used from time to time by Mrs. Day until the early 1930s). George Jackson built the fine three-story pink brick house (with corners of white sandstone) about one-half mile north of the Day home. (A good view of this pretty structure is had as we pass by on highway 550.) In 1914, Ouray County acquired the house along with thirty surrounding acres and established the County Poor Farm, which use continued until 1937 when it was bartered away in a three-way trade involving the State Department of Highways, Ouray County and a private land owner. Poor Farms were going out of fashion all over the nation at that time in favor of more modern means of accomplishing their purpose.

The boom and failure of the Chipeta scheme did not influence the town of Portland very much one way or another, for it already had a post office, school, two stores, a saloon, several other small shops and businesses and a population of 300. The town began to die slowly, however, for with nearby towns both to the south and north served by the railroad, Portland

At the time of the booming of the Ramona-Chipeta townsite, George Jackson built this fine two-and-a-half-story brick home. The corners, as well as windowsills, window lintels and door lintels, were of quarried, dressed limestone. In 1914, the County of Ouray acquired the house along with thirty acres to be used as the County Poor Farm. In 1937, it reverted again to private ownership when newer methods of caring for the county's indigent oldsters were adopted. (Doris H. Gregory)

was left at a considerable disadvantage. The post office was discontinued in 1896 but reestablished in 1900. However, during the four-year period of dormancy, another post office in Fremont County had been given the designation of Portland, therefore, the reborn post office at Portland was given the name "Plumer," the name of one of the founders and a prominent citizen. This new post ofice functioned for a year and a half only to be closed down again, this time—forever.

In 1975, a new Colorado law erased all the old townsites (Portland, Dallas, Red Mountain, Ironton and Sneffels) which didn't have a large population anymore and declared them to be "non-towns." We still have our memories though and if you live here a little while, you will learn that just a little piece down the road, at the junction of state Highway 23 with U.S. Highway 550 is "Portland."

Eight tenths of a mile further is Cedar Hill Cemetery. It was established in the 1870s. Some of the monuments have dates as old as 1878. The cemetery was used on an informal basis for almost twenty years before it was taken over by, surveyed, platted and run by the City of Ouray. It was known jokingly for some time as "Rowan's Farm" after the local Ouray doctor W.W. Rowan. Some areas of the cemetery are very well kept, but others are badly overgrown. There are many children's graves. The cemetery covers over fourteen acres. In 1948 the Cedar Hill Cemetery District took over operation of the area.

A short distance from Ridgway, the Lopa Hot Springs is just west of the road. The springs were originally used by the Ute Indians who believed it to be enchanted. Indian legend told that once there was a geyser here. Calcium sulfate and lime make up the bulk of sediments in the water with iron oxide giving it a reddish tinge. It comes out of the ground at close to 130 degrees. Ernest Ingersoll reports in 1883 that he "passed a copious spring of hot mineral water, carrying much iron, as we could tell by the circular tank of ferric oxide it has built around it, forming a bath large enough for a hundred persons at once. As yet there are few arrangements for making use of this fountain—a fact due to the plentiful hot springs of iron and of sulphur (sulfate of lime, etc.) water close to Ouray, where a sanitarium and bathhouses have been fitted up, and where persons suffering from rheumatism and kindred ailments find great benefit. So much warm water is poured into the Uncompahgre, in fact, that nothing more than a film of ice forms upon it in the coldest weather. Remembering all these varied advantages, it is no wonder the Utes loved the place and protested against its loss."

The area became the site of the Orvis Plunge and Orvis dancehall. The remains of the building still stand with the chimneys at each end of the building. L. F. Orvis constructed the bathhouse in the summer of 1919 and it became a popular resort with its immense supply of hot water.

At the Ridgway Rodeo, this cowboy stayed aboard his Brahma (cowboys pronounce it bray-ma) bull long enough for Art Fox to get this shot. The clowns are not there just to entertain the spectators, they distract the bull when the cowboy lands flat (as he often does) long enough to allow him to get on his feet. At least that gives him a running chance against an angry bull. (Art Fox)

In a little less than a mile and a half, the road joins with Colorado 62 which takes one over the Uncompahgre River and into Ridgway. To the south are the Ouray County Rodeo and Fairgrounds where events are held over Labor Day weekend. The rodeo was started in 1920 and includes a fair with extremely fine 4H exhibits. The rodeo began as a picnic for oldtimers held at Hohl's Grove-about four miles south of Ridgway on the river. In 1920, cattlemen joined in and held a rodeo at Ridgway. In the beginning, participants were mainly locals, but now the rodeo participants are almost all traveling professionals.

The Town of Ridgway itself is covered in Chapter 12, but by traveling over where the old railroad tracks crossed Highway 62 and then cutting back to the south one can go back to Ouray on what used to be the railroad right-of-way. As you leave Ridgway you will be passing the old railroad yard to the east. Near the city limits, the railroad platform is visible to the east of the road. The road southward out of Ridgway is not on the railroad bed but parallels it part of the time and even crosses it once or twice. At the point where the road branches to the right to lead through Idlewild and the Black Lake area, we begin traveling on the rail bed itself. We can follow the exact route of the train (for the most part) all the way into Ouray, keeping west of the river.

Two miles north of Ouray, Corbett Creek comes down from the west. A fatal wreck on the railroad happened at this site when a crew let a car get away at the Ouray Switchyards. They chased it with the engine running backwards towards Ridgway, but at this point the car and engine jumped the track and the fireman was killed. Corbett Creek has also been subject to flash floods which sometimes covered the tracks disrupting service. On the north side of the creek is the Dallas Trail, which leads up past several mines to within a half mile of the Whitehouse summit and then over to the Dallas area. Whitehouse Mountain and Moonshine Park are best seen from the other side of the canyon from the Dexter Creek Road. Whitehouse rises to 13,492 feet. The top part of the mountain is the only area in Ouray where three periods of volcanic activity can be seen. The San Juan Volcanic Series circles the bottom of the top cliffs with thin bands of Silverton Volcanic Series above. Most of the top of the mountain is Potosi Volcanic Series. The mountain makes up the northeast corner of the Sneffels range. Some geologists think that at one time gold veins stretched from Gold Hill to Whitehouse and that large amounts of gold must therefore have been washed out by glaciers and the Uncompahgre River. In fact, some gold has been found downstream in the river but very little has been found in the Whitehouse area. Only an experienced and well provisioned climber should try to make it all the way to the top of Whitehouse.

The Little Gem and Ben Hur are two of the mines in the area. The Little Gem was worked for several years in the 1890s by M.W. Quick. Some ore was taken out but it never proved out. In heavy timber, almost directly across on the south side of Corbett Creek from the Little Gem, is the Ben Hur. A small cabin was built in the area and the mine has been worked off and on since the 1890s.

Just a tenth of a mile further south was the site of the Mill Trestle. The extensive foundations of the smelter can still be seen by the river. This was a pyritic smelter with a 350-tons-per-day capacity, making it one of the largest smelters in the San Juans. It was owned by The Ouray Smelting and Refining Company. Thomas B. Crawford was president. It

Ouray Smelting and Refining Company's pyritic smelter, built at the river's edge two miles north of Ouray just north of Bachelor Switch. The smelter stood intact until torn down for the scrap metal it could provide during World War II. The "mill trestle" (foreground in front of the smelter) carried the mainline D&RG tracks. Two freight cars, seen at right, are set on a branch siding that served the smelter. (Denver Public Library)

was at sometime called the "Wanakah Smelter" for the Wanakah Mining Co. was in the smelting business too. The location made a long railroad trestle necessary to bypass it. It was powered by river water brought in by a quarter mile flume. An office building and several houses were located in the area. The smelter stood intact but unused for many years until World War II, when the building was stripped and razed for the scrap metal. The railroad continued to use the trestle until it, too, was scrapped in 1953. A tenth of a mile further, a bridge crosses the Uncompahgre. In the flat area southeast of this point, the railroad had a siding for loading ore from the Bachelor Mine and the area became known as the Bachelor Switch (elevation 7,580 feet). Later the railroad tried to name the area Lotus, but the name didn't take. Several railroad accidents also occurred at this spot. A passenger train once jumped the track with all six cars turning on their sides but there were no injuries. On another occasion, in 1909, a car load of ore got away from a switching crew and rolled north where it collided with a passenger train. Considerable damage was done to the engine and the car was demolished. Around $4,000 in Camp Bird ore (now worth twenty times as much) was shoveled into the river at the spot while clearing the wreck.

Traveling on south on the river road, one passes by the Silvershield or Wanakah Mill which used to be connected by tram to the American Nettie Mine, and the Wanakah Mine, both of which are highly visible perched on the top of the sheer cliffs across the canyon. "Silver Shield" was the name applied at the time of extensive remodeling in the years just after World War II. A trail leaves from the Silvershield and leads southwest up the steep cliffs to the Rock of Ages Mine and still further to

161

eventually tie in with the Twin Peaks Trail. The area was worked about 1910 or 1920 by a man named Harry Lewis. He mined by digging a meandering trench which still can be faintly seen. All ore was packed out on burros.

About two tenths of a mile south of the Silvershield Mill another trail works its way up the cliffs to the Grand View Mine. This mine was worked rather extensively and produced gold and iron pyrites. The Windam Co. seemed very optimistic about the mine in the 1880s and mentioned that it had just sold for $50,000. It was mined in the 1890s by two brothers from New York, W.F. and E.D. Mattes. They also built a mill at the base of the mountain and built a tram to carry down the ore. The mills' foundation can be seen to the right beside the road shortly before reaching the city and county maintenance buildings.

Shortly thereafter, on the west is a road leading to the Speedwell Mine. The area was worked in the 1890s by a St. Louis man named Bushman. It produced gold and the ore came down over a tram to the Skyrocket Mill on the other side of the canyon near the present day swimming pool. It soon shut down, but small amounts of additional work have been done over the years.

Away from the highways, small lakes are numerous in the mountains. Many of them are natural, having been formed either in volcanic craters (as is Como Lake) or by glacial action. Many have been enhanced by the addition of a dam or dike; some are entirely man-made, often for some mining or milling enterprise or for a community water supply. (Bill Fries III)

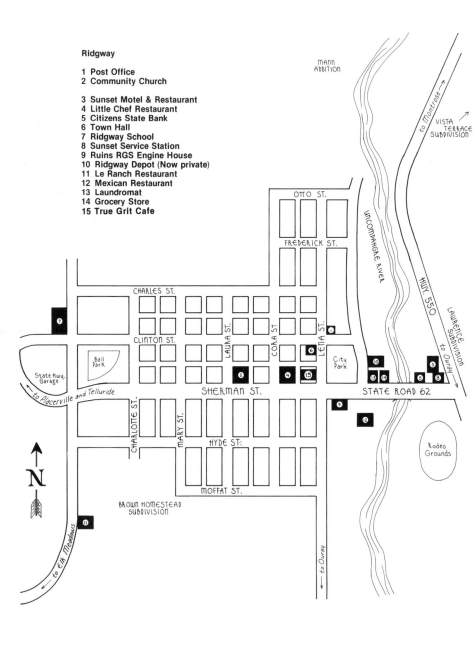

Ridgway

1 Post Office
2 Community Church

3 Sunset Motel & Restaurant
4 Little Chef Restaurant
5 Citizens State Bank
6 Town Hall
7 Ridgway School
8 Sunset Service Station
9 Ruins RGS Engine House
10 Ridgway Depot (Now private)
11 Le Ranch Restaurant
12 Mexican Restaurant
13 Laundromat
14 Grocery Store
15 True Grit Cafe

MANN ADDITION

to Montrose

VISTA TERRACE SUBDIVISION

OTTO ST.

FREDERICK ST.

CHARLES ST.

CLINTON ST.

LAURA ST.

CORA ST.

LENA ST.

HWY 550

LAWRENCE SUBDIVISION

to Ouray

UNCOMPAHGRE RIVER

Ball Park

City Park

State Hwy. Garage

to Placerville and Telluride

SHERMAN ST.

STATE ROAD 62

CHARLOTTE ST.

MARY ST.

HYDE ST.

Rodeo Grounds

N

MOFFAT ST.

BROWN HOMESTEAD SUBDIVISION

to Elk Meadows

to Ouray

CHAPTER 12
Town of Ridgway
R is for Railroad

Ridgway's birth is clouded in controversy. It was built at an elevation of 7,003 feet in the Uncompahgre Valley by several of the owners of the Rio Grande Southern Railroad. Some say the new town came about because Dave Wood (who owned large acreages around the town of Dallas three miles north) wanted to make a killing, some say because the owners of the RGS wanted to make a killing, and some say because it was the logical spot for extensive railroad facilities. By January 1890 the fact that a new town would be started was known to all. The town was rumored by the Ouray Daily News in February 2, 1890 to be called Magentie, then McGinty and later to be called Jordan, but it was generally established as Dallas Junction by March 1890. Most of the buildings in the old town of Dallas were moved there. In late March lots were selling for $300 to $500. The name was probably then later changed to avoid confusion with the old town of Dallas and to honor R. M. Ridgway. For awhile it was called Ridgway Junction. On June 6, 1890, the town was surveyed by George Hurlburt as the Ridgway Town Site (organized May 22, 1890) with a plat filed July 7, 1890. Otto Mears, Frederich Walson, Charles N. Nix and D.C. Hartwell organized the Ridgway Townsite Company. Streets running east-west are named after the founders and their male relatives. Streets running north-south are named after female relatives of the founders. Amos Walther eventually bought the company. He ended up donating the school grounds as well as the railroad shop, office and roundhouse grounds. Hall, in his 1890 history of Colorado, reported that "an effort is being made to build up a strong and substantial place. Several stores and residences have been erected, a large hotel built, a weekly newspaper established." By November 1890, the town was well under way. The depot, Mears Building, railroad buildings, hotel, saloon and the city's waterworks were almost finished. The Rio Grande Southern was to finish the link to the outside world which Telluride, Rico and Ophir so desperately needed. The railroad had been incorporated on November 5, 1889 and actual construction had been begun by Otto Mears on April 25, 1890. As the railroad grew so did the town. But then disaster struck. The Silver Panic of 1893 forced the RGS into receivership on August 2, 1893. Men were laid off and there was a substantial 20% lowering of most of the men's wages. The Denver and Rio Grande effectively obtained control of the RGS when its president, E.T. Jeffery, was appointed receiver because of the large bond holdings of the Denver & Rio Grande in the RGS. The RGS never again gained the glory of its first years and many of the towns it served never fully recovered either. The town of Ridgway

Town of Ridgway, looking southeast. Present-day Highway 550 and the Uncompahgre River lie just beyond the town. The road in the foreground is now Highway 62 that leads from Ridgway toward Dallas Divide (a paved road and a beautiful scenic drive). Ridgway, the town that the Rio Grande Southern built, has had some lean years since the demise of both the RGS and D&RG branch railroad. The completion of the Ridgway dam seems certain to give Ridgway a new lease on life. (Colorado Historical Society)

Rio Grande Southern roundhouse at Ridgway. Here, engines and cars were serviced and repaired. Here too, is the birthplace of the famous "Galloping Goose," a hybrid offspring of a railroad car and an automobile. Railroad "geneticists" experimented, first with a cross of Buick and railcar, then a cross with a Pierce-Arrow (the real classic), while a GMC truck and a Ford V8 also entered the equation at one time or another. (Denver Public Library)

struggled to grow. From 245 inhabitants in 1900, it grew to 376 in 1910 and 400 in 1920. A period followed during which the D & RG (now the Denver & Rio Grande Western) drained the line, finally ending in another receivership in 1929. The town's population dropped sharply to 239. But with the D & RG no longer bleeding the railroad, it began to recover and eventually the Galloping Goose was born. By 1940 the town had rebounded to a population of 354.

As stated, Ridgway was named for R.M. Ridgway, Superintendent of the mountain division of the Denver and Rio Grande. Ridgway loaned Mears equipment and was in charge generally of the railroad and specifically of the Ridgway to Rico construction of the RGS. Ridgway was born in New Jersey on September 13, 1835. He built and maintained track and bridges for the Union Army during the Civil War. (In 1881 he became superintendent of the D & RG's 3rd and 4th Divisions - mostly mountain). In 1892 Ridgway left the RGS, but he worked for the D & RG until 1902 when he retired. He never actually lived in the town.

The RGS was the early heart of the town's economy employing about 50 men at its home base in Ridgway. Originally the shops, a six-stall roundhouse, turntable, blacksmith shop, storeroom and water tank were located on forty acres purchased by the railroad to the northwest of the town. When they burned, a brick roundhouse and a two-story brick building for offices and shops were built in 1906 on land donated by Amos E. Walther. The roundhouse was a very large structure that could easily hold six locomotives at any given time. The depot was built in October 1890. A large icehouse of 1,000 tons capacity was also built to supply ice for perishable items, crew and passengers. At one time the RGS had 42 engines in operation. Most of the engines were nicknamed "Little Giants" as they weighed 30 tons, but could pull up to 25 cars loaded with up to 10 tons each. In 1919 the stockyards were moved from Dallas to the north part of town and Ridgway became a shipping point for stock as well as for ore from the mines.

The Ridgway depot was built and used by both the D & RG and the RGS. It cost $5,000 and opened October 24, 1890. It still stands, although moved from its original location at the east end of Clinton Street to a spot to the east of the old tracks. On the workshop site there were storeyards to the south, then going north were the turntable, roundhouse, storehouses and the office. The famous Galloping Goose was built here in the RGS shops - the first, in 1931, was an old Buick with a truck bed on railroad wheels. The Galloping Goose (called Puddle Jumper in its earlier days) was a unique contraption - half auto and half train brought about by a drop in passenger and freight business. The best known was a box car grafted to a 1926 Pierce Arrow sedan that could carry six to eight passengers and up to 10,000 pounds of freight. They ran daily beginning June 1931 between Ridgway and Durango, covering the 175 miles in a little less than nine hours (if there were no derailments, snowslides, breakdowns, etc.) One Goose is still on display in Telluride. A very good description of the various "Gooses" and their exploits is given in the Colorado Rail Annual, No. 9 published by the Railroad Museum at Golden, Colorado. They were discontinued from regular service in April 1950 but took a few persons on excursions in 1951. Service had been going downhill for a decade. Many of the mines closed when the price of zinc fell, the equipment and track were getting old and out of repair (causing many delays) and then, after World War II, a death blow was dealt when a $20-per-car surcharge was added to the freight charges. Customers began using trucks to ship their products. In March 1950, the railroad lost its mail contract because of high cost and inconsistent service. In 1951 the Idarado Mine at Pandora and the Argentine Mine at Rico switched to trucks for hauling their ore. Four hundred carloads of sheep, which were moved in the fall of 1951, were about the line's only

The D&RG Depot at Ridgway. After the bankruptcy of the Rio Grande Southern (caused by the collapse of silver mining in 1893) and the appointment of the D&RG as receiver, the depot served both railroads jointly. (Denver Public Library)

traffic. On April 15, 1951 the line was formally abandoned and by winter of 1953 the rails were torn up. The Rio Grande Southern was officially abandoned in 1951. In 1954 the D&RG narrow gauge from Montrose to Ridgway was replaced with a broad gauge. That track was abandoned and torn up in 1977 and 1978.

Unfortunately, many of Ridgway's buildings have been destroyed by fire (most of which occurred in the 1930s). The most famous hotel in town was the Mentone, built by D.C. Hartwell who was also one of six men who promoted and built the Beaumont Hotel in Ouray. It cost $40,000

The famed Galloping Goose poses for its picture. No. 7 was powered by a 1936 Ford V8 engine in a 1926 Pierce-Arrow "33" body. (Denver Public Library)

The Mentone Hotel. Built with greater optimism than later circumstances warranted. Tourist traffic never justified its size. At least some of its builders were from the same group who organized the RGS Railroad and the town of Ridgway. D.C. Hartwell, among them, was also one of the builders of the Beaumont Hotel in Ouray. The Mentone was destroyed by fire in the mid 1930s. (Gladys Fournier)

The heart of downtown Ridgway, 1912 or 1913. Motor traffic is quite heavy, considering the year. Looking east, the D&RG Depot is seen at the far end of the street. (Ruth Gregory Collection)

and had 55 rooms on three floors. It had a dining room and the bank was originally located here. An attempt was made in 1905 to rob the hotel's safe. A trench was dug and an attempt made to blow the safe. The hotel burned down in 1935. Early day pictures of the town were so dominated by the hotel that one can hardly tell it's the same town. Many dances were held and many of the railroad men boarded at the hotel (the Mentone supplied lunch box meals for the men).

Ridgway was a typical Western town because of the large ranching operations carried on in the area. The cowboys would come in and tie their horses to the hitching rail for a Saturday night of fun on the town. Gunfights and horse races were often seen. At one time, as many as five saloons operated in the town including the Mentone Hotel Bar, Bob Low's Saloon, Palmer Saloon, Quist's Saloon and one other. Nichols' and Fisher's livery stable was one of the first businesses established in the new town. Later Nichols and Robinson started the Ridgway Transfer and Auto Line in 1912.

The first school in Ridgway was held in the Binder Blacksmith Shop and later in the Mentone Hotel. The first real schoolhouse was built in 1899 and was a two-story elementary school near the south edge of town. It was injured by an earthquake in the early 1900s. In 1908 a high school was added. In 1915 the school was located in the Hotchkiss Building and in 1920 in the City Hall. In 1931 the grade school burned down and the Park Hotel was used until a new building was built in 1934. In the 1970s, the present school was constructed.

The Ridgway Community Church was built as the Methodist Church in 1903 at a cost of $3,000 and with a seating capacity of 300. In 1913 fire did a little damage to the roof of the church. In 1930, the bell was purchased, with half the cost being borne by the Ridgway Fire Department which used it for fires. Fire damaged the church in 1936.

The Ridgway flour mill was built about 1890 to the east of the town by D.C. Hartwell. It cost about $15,000 and had a capacity of about 50 barrels a day. For several decades it was one of the main industries of the town. An electric light plant was built to light the facility. It closed about 1910. The flour mill was later converted to the county garage and storage building.

A great disaster shook the town on January 6, 1957 when the garage and shed caught fire. The fire department and many spectators rushed to the site only to have dynamite explode, killing 3 and injuring 18. Windows were broken for half a mile around and the 2½-story building disintegrated.

The Ridgway City Park was named for D.C. Hartwell who laid out the square and was one of the original founders. Many trees have been planted in the park as well as other parts of town. It is a favorite picnicking spot.

The creamery (which still stands) was erected in 1905 and operated by George W. Branman. It gradually built up to a capacity of about 7,000 pounds of butter a week. It produced a very good product that was in great demand in the area.

The Park Hotel (1911 photo). The hotel was located where the Ridgway Town Hall is now, just across the street from the town park. The railroad tracks and depot are in view across the park. The Park Hotel really put on the dog with its uniformed maids, waitresses, etc. The man with the soiled apron must be the chef. (Ouray County Historical Society)

The two-story Mears building is still located on a corner facing the park. It was originally to be frame, but when it blew down during construction it was changed to brick. The second floor of the building was used by the RGS for offices until 1907 when an office building was built near the new roundhouse after fire destroyed the old buildings. The Ridgway Post Office operated under the direction of Mr. H.P. Ede who also had a small store.

Ridgway's first newspaper was "The Populist," published by J.P. Cassidy in the 1890s. E.C. Bacon and Curtis Wright also published the Ridgway Herald. However, the town's major newspaper was the Ridgway Sun which produced its first issue on August 29, 1908. Grant Turner was the publisher. It was a Republican newspaper run by Turner, his wife and son. The newspaper's press ran on a gasoline engine that caused a terrible racket and annoyed the neighbors. The paper was started with the promise that it would get all of the RGS printing, but its fortunes declined along with those of the railroad.

The Ridgway Bank, started by A.E. Walther, had resources of $60,000 in 1907. In 1917 new owners took over. In 1931 the bank folded when C.M. Stanwood embezzled bank money to play the stock market (he figured the market was as low as it would go and was bound to come up soon). He was tried, convicted and sentenced to 17 to 20 years in prison.

Several motion pictures have been made in or near Ridgway including "How the West Was Won," "Tribute to a Bad Man" and "True Grit." Several buildings were built at those times and other buildings have been altered to fit a movie. Many of the buildings around the square still carry signs painted for "True Grit."

For a long time in the 1960s and 1970s it was thought the town would be under water when the Dallas Dam was built, but in 1976 the area that the dam project was to cover was lessened and now the lake begins about three miles north of the town. Ridgway now looks forward to a bright future with anticipated growth due to the closeness of the new lake.

Former Ridgway Post Office (August 1, 1911 photo). The building is still standing although the facade at the top is gone and its appearance is altered so as to make it unrecognizable. (Ouray County Historical Society)

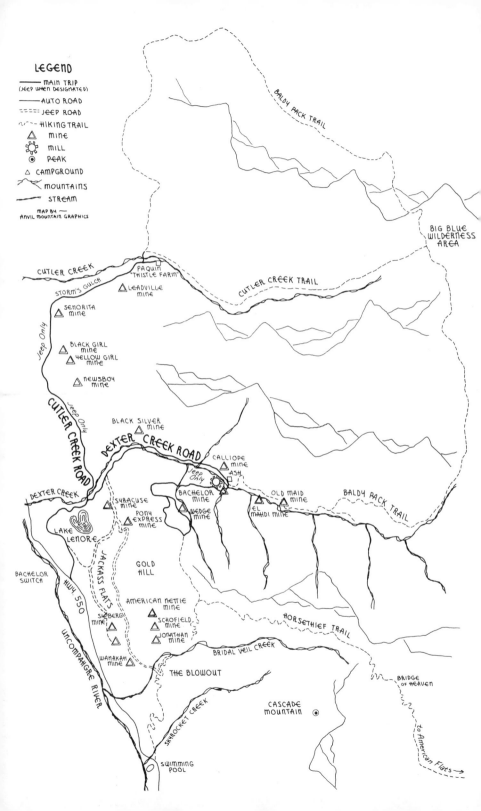

LEGEND
MAIN TRIP (JEEP WHEN DESIGNATED)
AUTO ROAD
JEEP ROAD
HIKING TRAIL
△ MINE
✳ MILL
◉ PEAK
△ CAMPGROUND
⋀⋀ MOUNTAINS
∿ STREAM
MAP BY —
ANVIL MOUNTAIN GRAPHICS

BALDY PACK TRAIL

BIG BLUE WILDERNESS AREA

CUTLER CREEK

STORM'S GULCH

PAQUIN THISTLE FARM

LEADVILLE MINE

CUTLER CREEK TRAIL

SENORITA MINE

Jeep Only

BLACK GIRL MINE
YELLOW GIRL MINE

NEWSBOY MINE

CUTLER CREEK ROAD

Jeep Only

BLACK SILVER MINE

DEXTER CREEK ROAD

CALLIOPE MINE
ASH

Jeep Only

BACHELOR MINE

OLD MAID MINE

DEXTER CREEK

BALDY PACK TRAIL

SYRACUSE MINE

EL MAHDI MINE

PONY EXPRESS MINE

WEDGE MINE

LAKE LENORE

BACHELOR SWITCH

HWY 550

JACKASS FLATS

GOLD HILL

AMERICAN NETTIE MINE

HORSETHIEF TRAIL

SIOBERG MINE

SCHOFIELD MINE

JONATHAN MINE

UNCOMPAHGRE RIVER

WANAKAH MINE

BRIDAL VEIL CREEK

BRIDGE OF HEAVEN

THE BLOWOUT

CASCADE MOUNTAIN ◉

SKYROCKET CREEK

to American Flats →

SWIMMING POOL

CHAPTER 13
Dexter and Cutler Creek Roads
Three Bachelors Make a Mine

The first mile of road on this trip is now a county road and a car can travel most of the lower part of the route. There is a considerable amount of private property in the area (three subdivisions - Pineview, Panoramic Heights and Lake Lenore - and a private lake).

Traveling 3/10th of a mile up the road a small (now impassible) trail is visible to the right. This trail used to lead to the Memphis Mine and Jackass Flats, but is now impassible to all but foot traffic. One tenth of a mile further along the road to the left is the foundation of the Banner American Mill. It was owned by G. A. Franz Sr. and his sons, G. A. Franz II (Bud - who was a mining engineer and directed operation of several mines being operated and producing ore for the mill), Richard K. Franz (superintendent for the mill operations), and Oscar (the third son and the youngest who didn't have a chance to participate in the family enterprise all that much). The Franz money was largely dissipated, operating mines and milling ore at a time when the market wouldn't provide sufficient return. During the worst part of the depression of the 1930s, the Franz's supported the largest payroll in the Ouray area and were credited by many with "keeping Ouray afloat." During World War II, after G. A. Franz Sr. had died, the Franz mines were not yielding a profit and money for additional development was lacking. The sons sold the mill to the American Lead-Zinc, who leased several mines in the area and milled the ore there. That operation, too, ceased not long after the end of the war.

Bud Franz (now retired) was subsequently Deputy Commissioner of Mines for many years. Richard was, for many years, mill operator for the Idarado Mill at Telluride. O. E. (Oscar), the youngest of the Franz brothers, has been an official of the Colorado Public Utilities Commission. A portion of Panoramic Heights has been built on tailings from this mill.

A short distance further the road enters the Lake Lenore area which is private property. The lake was originally called Mannon's Lake. George Wettengel bought it and changed its name. Wettengel was a nephew of A. W. Begole, one of the founders of Ouray. He came here to work for the Begole Mercantile shortly after the sale of the Mineral Farm Mine. Wettengel had been, at one time, owner and operator of the "Temple of Music," a bawdy-house on 2nd Street. When Colorado went dry in 1916, such places as the Temple of Music were forced to close. Wettengel's attempt to develop a "country club" at Lake Lenore failed, perhaps because the local bootleggers had not gotten organized and into full production yet. Jack McMahon, part owner and manager of the Wedge Mine lived here, but when his wife and niece drowned in the lake he left the area. It is now a private subdivision.

At the fork, the road to the right leads through aspen and spruce to the Bachelor Mine and the ghost town of Ash. The road to the left leads past three old large mines in semi-arid country and then passes into dense pine, spruce and aspen with several hiking trails and small streams.

Taking the left fork, it will be approximately half a mile until you are out of private property. At this point a barely passible private jeep road leaves to the right and climbs for half a mile to the Newsboy Mine (first called the Still). The Newsboy still has a beautiful boardinghouse standing. The Newsboy was opened about 1890 and produced mainly silver.

Traveling down the road a cattle guard divides private property from forest service land. The road leaving to the left is the old Cutler Creek Road and it is not suggested for travel as it is a difficult road that leads to nowhere interesting.

About one half mile past the cattle guard on the east side of the road is the Senorita Mine. A cabin and several crumbly ruins still stand. The mine has been worked off and on for many years. Azurite (a blue carbonate of copper) and malachite (a green copper carbonate) are found in abundance at this mine and at the Black Girl Mine. The Black Girl Mine is located about a quarter mile down the old road leading from the Senorita back to the south toward Ouray. The area was not seriously

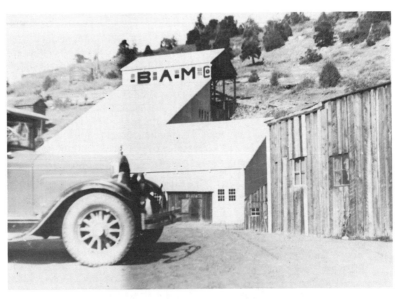

Banner American Mill. A housing development, known as Panoramic Heights, now occupies the former site of the Banner American Mill, built in the early 1930s and in operation until the end of World War II. It was owned and operated by the Franz family: G.A. Franz Sr., G.A. (Bud) Franz II and Richard K. Franz. A younger brother, O. E. Franz, was busy being a student and serving in the military during those years. Many folk in Ouray credited the Franz enterprise with keeping Ouray alive during the worst of the depression years; at that time, they had the largest payroll in the county. (Ruth Gregory Collection)

worked until about 1900 and then not worked for long. The Yellow Girl Mine was also part of this property and lies directly above the Black Girl.

Shortly after the road passes the Senorita it enters the forest. This area was named Storm's Gulch (possibly after a local sawmill owner). Cutler Creek flows down the middle of the gulch and a small park is at the east end. The ranch in the park sits on forest service land. It is most often called Thistle Farm although a number of different people have lived on the property over the years. The Thistles grew acres of strawberries. At one time a small town called Camp Paquin was also in the area (the area is in the Paquin Mining district). An early road (constructed before 1887) used to come up from Portland on the north side of Cutler Creek. Early maps showed half a dozen cabins in the area.

The road crosses Cutler Creek at which point the South Fork Trail and Baldy Trail leave to the right. About a tenth of a mile further is a nice campground area and a tenth of a mile above that, where the road crosses the creek, is the North Cutler or Zig Zag Trail and Cobbs Gulch. This trail follows the creek for a quarter mile then turns west. It is not advisable to take a car up the road past this point as the road dead-ends after 7/10ths of a mile at a spot where it is almost impossible to turn around. North Fork Trail is 4.4 miles long and South Fork is 2.9 miles in length. Baldy Trail is about 5 miles, making a full trip almost ten miles. The trails are rather steep and climb the ridge that separates the Cow Creek and Uncompahgre River drainages. Although the trails may not sound long, it is a good idea to allow at least one full day, and preferably two, to take these hikes. The area is a favorite hunter access point in the fall. Major parts of the hike are in the Big Blue Wilderness area and make good horseback as well as pack trails.

Going back to the Lake Lenore area, the other road starts off to the east following Dexter Creek (also known as Red Canyon Creek). This is a favorite path for snowmobilers and cross country skiers in winter. A short distance above the fork, a road leads off to the right to Jackass Flats and the Blowout area which are covered at the end of this chapter.

A half mile further south is a small cabin to the left side of the road. It is presumed that this was living quarters for the Black Silver Mine which is about half way up the mountain on the other side of Dexter Creek. The Windham report in 1880 reported that the mine had a high grade smelting ore and that the shaft had been sunk 60 feet.

A mile further is the site of the ghost town of Ash. Ash existed because of the Bachelor Mine on the south side of Dexter Creek and the Calliope Mine on the north. Both mines produced high grade silver ore in the 1890s. The Bachelor eventually produced in excess of $3,500,000. The Calliope group included the Dexter, Iowa and Chief mines. A post office was established at Ash and at its high point around 300 people lived in the area. The town derived its name from the last names of the persons who owned the Bachelor Mine at that time (Armstrong, Sanders and Hurlburt). Although now quickly reached, the town then was approximately a half-day trip from Ouray thus creating a need for a settlement. Many workers at the mine or mill that had families built cabins in the area. C.W. Cornforth & Son made daily trips from Ouray with a four-horse team to carry mail and supplies.

The Bachelor Mine derived its name from the three men who discovered it as all were unmarried at the time. The mine has almost always produced profitably and, in the 1890s, was one of the greatest silver producers in the area. The vein was thought to be formed by cavity filling with some replacement. The mine has a main tunnel of over 700 feet with drifts of up to 1,000 feet. Veins of over 4,500 feet have been found in the area. The Wedge and Neodesha mines (1,500 and 3,500 feet away) are on the same vein. The main vein was struck in 1892. The total output of the mine had exceeded $2,000,000 in the first twelve years after its discovery. During the mine's heyday, some pockets of ore were found with as much as 15,000 ounces of silver per ton (almost 50% solid silver). The mines are still being worked off and on. Armstrong eventually bought out his two partners and built a mill on the north side of the creek. A trestle ran across the creek and the mill operated for several more years. Hurlburt used his money from the sale of the mine to buy the Grizzly Bear Mine on Bear Creek.

The Calliope (or Dexter Mine) was on the north side of the creek - although later surveys showed that the claim probably went to the south side of the creek and that part of the Bachelor dump and boardinghouse were probably on Calliope property. The mine was worked in the 1880s and produced silver averaging 100 ounces per ton. Adam Herzinger located the Calliope in 1880, but Charles Nix soon owned a controlling three-fourths interest. The mine was most profitable in its early years. Most of the tunnels have now caved in and are overgrown by brush. All the buildings in the Calliope area have been torn down for the lumber. The area is a good one for hunting.

If you follow a foot path directly alongside the north side of Dexter Creek you will be on the Baldy Trail. The beginning of the trail is hard to follow, but after a few hundred yards you will come to a large draw. Go to the left up the draw a short way until you see the trail looping back south. A huge hole in the ground marks the spot of the Almadi and Old Maid mines. Several old cabins are in the area. The trail winds around several ridges for about ten miles before ending at Cutler Creek.

If you go across Dexter Creek at the Bachelor you are on a road about one and a half miles long going up through a deep spruce forest, into an aspen forest and leading to the Wedge Mine. There are several side roads as the whole area back to the southwest is covered with small tunnels, collapsed cabins, large dumps and overgrown trails. There is a trail leading from a small meadow along the road above the Wedge which ties in two miles away with Horsethief Trail. Horsethief Trail is a very old trail. It was used in early days by thieves who stole horses from the San Luis Valley and then took them to Utah for resale. It was used even earlier than that by the Ute Indians who also probably transported stolen goods. The trail offers some of the most beautiful and spectacular scenery in the area, but it is a very hard one-day hike and it will take most people two days or more to travel it. It is a good, although scary, horseback ride. Many have called this the most scenic trail in America. The trail used to begin at the swimming pool in Ouray but was closed due to neglect. The trail passes through aspen, then spruce, then goes above tree line. Ouray becomes visible far down below.

About four miles up the trail is the Bridge of Heaven, a narrow hogback only six to seven feet wide with drops almost 3,000 feet on each side, from an elevation of 12,308 feet. Crags and canyons are everywhere. Fantastic views of Whitehouse, Potosi and Abrams can be had. Grand Mesa is visible 80 miles to the north. Inexperienced horseback riders should lead their steeds over this part of the trail! Bighorn Sheep often can be seen along this ridge.

Bachelor Mine, up Dexter Creek Road. The founders and developers of this mine were Armstrong, Sanders and Hurlbert. The community that grew around this camp, using the three initials of the owners, became "ASH," the post office designation. In defiance of the best geological advice, the owners of the Bachelor went their own way—and struck it rich! (Denver Public Library)

Riders silhouetted against the sky as they thread their way across the "Bridge Of Heaven" on the Horse Thief Trail. Riding single file (they have to) riders cross over the narrow ridge on their way toward the top of the Amphitheatre (above Ouray) and beyond into American Flats. (Ruth Gregory Collection)

179

The trail then runs east and southeast to a grassy level spot known as American Flats. The trail reaches almost 12,700 feet at Wildhorse Pass. Wildhorse Peak (elevation 13,268 feet) is about 1½ miles to the west. Near this point the trail forks off several ways, one leading down Bear Creek for three miles to Highway 550 and another leading eastward 26

Looking north toward Ridgway, the Uncompahgre River may be seen on the valley floor at left. At upper right, very black against the sky, is the bunkhouse for the American Nettie Mine. The small building extending beyond the cliff a bit is the latrine with a water-less sanitary system—very practical. (Colorado Historical Society)

The American Nettie Mill, west of the Uncompahgre River, across the valley from "Gold Hill" upon whose cliffs is the American Nettie Mine. Ore was delivered from mine to mill by means of an aerial tramway that made a descent of 1,820 feet in two spans totalling 4,200 feet. The lower span that crossed the valley was 2,100 feet long and had a vertical drop of 915 feet. Only two buckets were used on the tram—one going down, one going up. (Ruth Gregory Collection)

miles to Lake City. Straight through the flats is the top of Engineer Pass. At this point Horsethief can be dangerous. It has been called a confusing wonderland that beguiles all unprotected strangers into the sinuosities of Cow Creek.

Going back down to slightly above Lake Lenore, a jeep or four-wheel-drive road leaves to the right. About a tenth of a mile up the road a small mill and mine are visible to the right. This is the site of the Syracuse Tunnel driven in the 1920s by the Bachelor Mine group. The tunnel was driven to strike the Bachelor vein at a lower level. Some good ore was found as the tunnel was driven and it did prove to be an easier way to get ore out of the Bachelor workings. A two-story boardinghouse was once located on the site but it was destroyed by fire. The mine is being worked as a very interesting mine tour at present.

Continuing on up the road for 3/10ths of a mile further, the road forks. The right fork goes to Jackass Flats and the Memphis Mine. Jackass Flats derived its name from the many burros that roamed wild over it. Most prospectors just turned their burros loose when they grew old or when the men quit prospecting. Now the area is often inhabited in the winter by small herds of mountain sheep. The road leads through the flats and out onto a shelf toward the Memphis Mine (the last half mile of the road is now washed out). Several buildings still stand.

The left fork of the road leads by the Pony Express dump. The mine itself can be reached only by climbing the steep slopes. The Pony Express was patented by H.R. Price in 1887. The mine has been worked off and on right up to recent times. The Pony Express limestone unit of the Wanakah formation (Jurassic Age) was named after the limestone taken from the mine. The Pony Express limestone is dark and shaley and since it was a carbonate it was an ideal site for ore deposit.

A little more than a mile further, the road passes the Sieburg Mine to the right. Sieburg Tunnel was at 8,685 feet and ran about 2,000 feet. It was driven to reach American Nettie ore. An interesting boardinghouse and equipment shed remain. A quarter of a mile south of the Sieburg, at the same elevation, is the Wanakah. This area was developed about 1910 by G.H. Barnhart. The name came from the Wanakah Club in Buffalo, New York, where most of the money was raised. The venture was meant to redevelop existing claims. The American Nettie Mill was purchased and the tram was remodeled to deliver Wanakah ore. For several years the ore was milled at a profit but when it began carrying heavy iron content the mill's equipment was not sufficient.

On up the road, near the top of what is called Gold Hill or Lookout Mountain, is the American Nettie Group. Beginning at the north is the Chipeta Tunnel which was driven in the 1890s by Walter Bunce on the belief that the American Nettie ore extended north.

The American Lode was the first located of the American Nettie group by John R. Porter and Thomas Nash on October 8, 1885. The Nettie and Schofield were located in November 1888 by W.B. Barringer and W.P. Conner. The American Lode sold in 1888 for $5,000. By January 1889 the group sold for $40,000 and by March of the same year it sold again for $43,000. The area's dumps were leased in March 1896 to Thomas Walsh. The claims spread all the way up the mountain to Horsethief Trail. The tram which was built from the mine to the mill on the valley floor when low grade ore began to be mined, was known as the highest in the world as the mine was situated nearly 1,800 feet above the river on the nearly perpendicular cliffs. It had only two buckets with the loaded one coming down while pulling the other up.

A steep trail began at the swimming pool area (then a fishpond) and was used for access. This trail was in continuous use until McCullough and Withrow ceased operations during World War II. Bulky items such as timber and rails could be transported only by burro trains that sometimes were a block long. The balance of the supplies went in the tram along with an occasional miner who might lean over the sides of the bucket or ride on the rim. The American Nettie became a very famous gold mine. By 1905 the mine had already produced $1,464,923 and more than ten miles of tunnels were driven into the mountain. Total production probably exceeded $2,000,000. Unlike many mines in the area, this was a dry mine (water never touched the miners). It was lighted by electricity (one of the first mines to use it) with the generator located on the Uncompahgre River. Ruby silver was also present in the mine and it was so brilliant that jets of water used to cool the miners' drill bits often ran blood red.

The Jonathon and Bright Diamond mines are located to the south of and below the American Nettie. They operated during the 1890s, but their deposits soon ran out. A mill was built in the valley just south of the present Elkhorn Hotel (in the Skyrocket Creek area) and a tram connected the two.

The area to the south of these mines is known as the Blowout. The name was given it by early miners, but it was not formed by volcanic activity rather by minerals being forced up by extreme pressures about 100 million years ago. It is a highly mineralized area and was heavily prospected since it lay close to town, but it was almost ten years after the town was founded that any large quantities of ore were found. Some beautiful scenery, including spectacular Bridal Veil Falls, is visible on up the road.

Many large buildings, such as the San Juan Chief Mill, never had a coat of paint. Yet, the San Juan Chief, without any maintenance or care, has required more than ninety years to bring it to this state of decay. Much of the lumber is still reasonably sound. This could not be in any area where the humidity is consistently high and where termites thrive. (Bill Fries III)

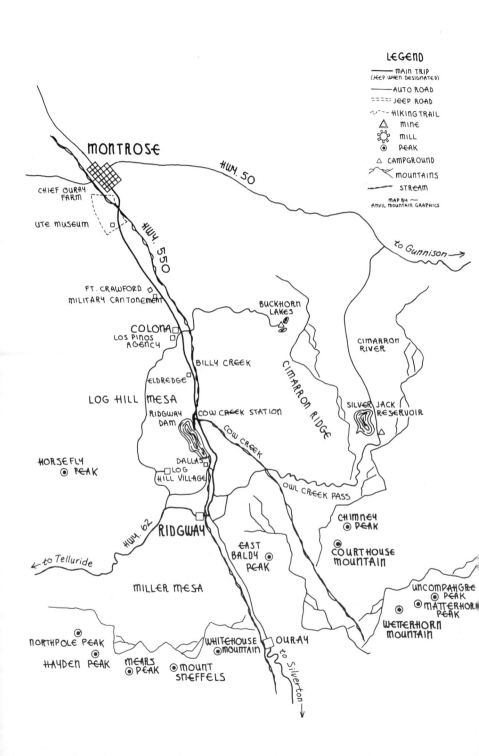

LEGEND

——— MAIN TRIP
(JEEP WHEN DESIGNATED)
———— AUTO ROAD
===== JEEP ROAD
~~~~ HIKING TRAIL
△ MINE
✿ MILL
◉ PEAK
△ CAMPGROUND
⋀ MOUNTAINS
——— STREAM

MAP BY —
ANVIL MOUNTAIN GRAPHICS

MONTROSE

HWY. 50

CHIEF OURAY FARM

UTE MUSEUM

HWY. 550

to Gunnison →

FT. CRAWFORD
MILITARY CANTONEMENT

BUCKHORN LAKES

COLONA
LOS PINOS AGENCY

BILLY CREEK

CIMARRON RIVER

CIMARRON RIDGE

ELDREDGE

LOG HILL MESA

RIDGWAY DAM

COW CREEK STATION

SILVER JACK RESERVOIR

COW CREEK

HORSEFLY
◉ PEAK

DALLAS
LOG HILL VILLAGE

OWL CREEK PASS

HWY. 62

RIDGWAY

← to Telluride

EAST BALDY PEAK

CHIMNEY
◉ PEAK

COURTHOUSE MOUNTAIN

MILLER MESA

UNCOMPAHGRE
◉ PEAK
◉ MATTERHORN PEAK

WETTERHORN MOUNTAIN

NORTHPOLE PEAK ◉

HAYDEN PEAK ◉

MEARS
◉ PEAK

WHITEHOUSE
◉ MOUNTAIN

OURAY

◉ MOUNT SNEFFELS

to Silverton ↓

CHAPTER 14
Ridgway to Montrose
Ranches and Railroading

Traveling north out of Ridgway on Highway 550, one passes through the lower elevations of Ouray County. The cutoff to Owl Creek Pass through the Cow Creek area is a series of dirt roads which are sometimes not open to regular automobiles in the winter. However, the roads are then excellent for snowmobiling and cross country skiing. In the summer, the main road travels about 30 miles over Cimarron Ridge (top elevation of road is about 10,000 feet) to Silver Jack Reservoir. It then continues down the Cimarron River to Highway 50 and connects at a point about half-way between Montrose and Blue Mesa Reservoir. This general route used to be called the Cimarron Cutoff Trail and was one of the early-day routes of travel from Lake City to Ouray. Otto Mears used parts of it as an early toll road.

The Cow Creek valley is a ranching area that has continuously produced large amounts of hay. The area also contains vast coal beds, some of which are as much as 72-feet-thick. Cow Creek received its name from the first white men who entered the area with cattle for the Ute Indian reservation. They picked this naturally bountiful area to graze them.

Courthouse Mountain and Chimney Peak (the sharpest large ridge) are easily visible from near Highway 550. Their jagged peaks were formed from Volcanic tuff. It is easy to determine where the names came from. To the left is Cimarron Ridge, called the Sawtooth Range by Ingersoll—"the outline of which I can only compare to the jagged confusion of the broken bottles set along the top of a stone wall." These mountains should be climbed only by the experienced rope climber. However, many trails lead into some of the most exciting mountain wilderness hiking and climbing areas in the San Juans. The area is very remote and it is suggested that reference be made to topographical maps or Robert Ormes Guide for further details. The U.S. Forest Service maintains many trails in the area, including Middle Fork #227, East Fork #228, Uncompahgre Peak #237, Wetterhorn Peak #233, Wetterhorn Basin #226, and Alpine Trail #225. All of the trails are long and lead into extremely isolated country. It is suggested that horses be used or that hikers be prepared to spend many days in the Big Blue Wilderness Area. Domestic and wild sheep abound in the high country. Several 14,000-feet peaks are near the end of the trails. Wetterhorn (14,015 feet) is a technical climb but Uncompaghre (14,309 feet) is extremely easy. It is a good practice to always take along the appropriate topographical maps. The Silver Jack Reservoir offers good fishing and there are many good camping areas along the Cimarron and alongside the lake. The 332-acre lake offers good bank fishing for small rainbows. No boats are allowed. All three forks of the Cimarron also offer good rainbow and brook trout fishing.

Courthouse Mountain and Chimney Rock as seen from one of the roads that lead into Cow Creek country (the Owl Creek Road leads to these landmarks). Excellent views of Courthouse Mountain may be seen from the plateau, west of Ridgway on Highway 62, from Dallas Divide and from Highway 550 about two miles north of Ridgway. Just beyond and obscured from view by Courthouse Mountain is the San Juan's highest—Uncompahgre Peak, 14,309 feet above the sea. (Bill Fries III)

Silver Jack Reservoir. Located on the Cimmaron side of Owl Creek Pass, it is named for the Silver Jack Mine which is up a side canyon in the vicinity. (Bill Fries III)

The town of Dallas was located about one-half mile north of the Cow Creek (Owl Creek cutoff). It was in and above the present-day field near the junction of Dallas Creek and the Uncompahgre River. Early Spanish trails from the Durango area led from the San Miguel River over to Dallas Creek and down to the Uncompahgre through what was originally called Unaweep Valley. It is therefore likely that the Spaniards panned for gold in the area. Before the Indians were removed to Utah the area was settled by gold placer miners who rushed in after a find. Sidney Jocknick, who lived in Dallas, reported that a city (originally called Unaweep and then Gold City) of tents sprung up in one day in 1879 when bars of placer gold were discovered at the junction of Dallas Creek and the Uncompahgre River. It lasted until "the summer season had blended with autumn...and the denizens of Gold City one fine morning in August packed up their 'dunnage' and pulled out for Rico." Dallas was within Indian territory. The Indians could not have been exactly overjoyed by the placering activities and the onrush of white men in 1879, or the later, more permanent settlement in 1880 and 1881. There is no evidence, however, that the Indians made any war-like feints in the direction of Dallas or even any threats of violence. In those years, relations were delicately balanced between the white man and the Indian and, indeed, it was the latter who was most anxious to maintain peace at that time. It is most likely that the town of Dallas didn't actually "take root" until after the banishment of the Utes in the autumn of 1881. Support for this theory lies in the fact that the town was not recognized at all by the U.S. Postal Department until February 11, 1884. At that time the post office was "moved" from Lawrence, where it had been in service only since February 5, 1883. The area was also called Dallas Junction or Dallas Station by some. In 1884, the area had a population of 100 and assumed the pretentious name of Dallas City. By 1887, two hotels, a saloon, a post office and grocery, stables and a blacksmith shop had been built along the toll road which ran through town and was called Dallas Avenue.

On August 24, 1887, when regular railroad service arrived, the town boomed. The area became the railroad's terminal for four months. David Day in the **Solid Muldoon** called it a "sinful city" because of the construction workers. "Horse racing, stallion poker, scarlet daughters and numerous other sin-breeding dives and nuisances" were in the city. On September 10, 1888, a fire started in the laundry in the back of the Dallas Hotel and burned the business district to the ground. The buildings were almost immediately built again. On February 7, 1889, the citizens voted to incorporate and the town became official on March 9, 1889. Some of the houses and the school were built along the west side of the river. There were two bridges and two footbridges across the rivers for access. One bridge was across the Uncompahgre just north of the junction with Dallas Creek. A half-mile race track was located near the city. In 1890, the town hit its peak population (541) due to the feverous activity associated with building the Rio Grande Southern Railroad.

After establishment of Ridgway (incorporated April 14, 1891) three miles south, the town began to decline. There is controversy over whether Dave Wood Sr. held out from the railroad or whether D & RG officers Mears, Hartwell and Walsen wanted to make their own killing by starting the new town of Ridgway for the railroad's shops. Perhaps Dave Wood was not anxious to favor the railroad at that point for it spelled the "end of the line" for his freighting business which he had built and operated for several years. However, it was very common in those days for an expanding railroad line to found townsites along their lines at points that would not only later serve the railroad's interests but would also be immediately profitable as businesses and residents moved in, bought lots, built and developed the towns. The site of Ridgway was a more logical and practical choice for the purposes of the Rio Grande Southern with a great deal more room for switchyards, roundhouse, depot and office buildings. Another fire hit Dallas in 1892 and the population declined to about 50. The post office was removed in October of 1899. By 1900, the area was all but a ghost town. Some fascinating stories about the society of the Town of Dallas can be found in Josie Crum's book **Ouray County, Colorado**. Her family lived on a ranch just north of town. In 1975, Dallas was officially abandoned as a town.

About seven miles further north was Eldredge, a stop on the Montrose-Ouray line at an elevation of 6,554 feet. It is located at Billy Creek about three miles after Highway 550 crosses the Uncompahgre

Main Street, Dallas, distant down the street, on the right, may be seen two canvas-covered wagons. It is probably safe to presume that they are some of David Wood's freight wagons for Dallas was his last forwarding point as the D&RG extended its rails—first Gunnison, then Montrose and finally Dallas. The rails were extended from Dallas to Ouray (there was no Ridgway yet). Discernible signs, from left, Saloon, Restaurant, Meat Market, Groceries, Montrose Merc's Branch House and above that building, the sign over the Dallas Hotel. Although Dallas was on the D&RG mainline to Ouray, it began to lose its dominant position in the valley when the Rio Grande Southern established the town of Ridgway in 1890. Today, nothing recognizable as a town remains.

River. In the 1870s and 1880s, small farms owned by the Ute Indian subchiefs were located in the area. Each farm had a small house.

Three more miles north of Eldredge is the town of Colona which lies just barely south of the Ouray and Montrose county line. Colona is Spanish for Colonist. It may have been called "Hotchkiss" for a brief time for Preston and Roswell Hotchkiss, who moved into the area shortly after the building of the D & RG railroad from Montrose to Ouray. However, there was already a town of "Hotchkiss" on the North Fork of the Gunnison River, founded by their brother Enos Hotchkiss in 1882. Preston and Roswell had been among the developers of Portland and had a ranch and a business there. A "Hotchkiss Addition" was added to the Town of Portland in 1886. They later had a business in Dallas and still later at Ridgway.

The town of Colona is almost on the precise site of the Los Pinos Agency, established in the fall of 1875, when the agency was moved from its former location on Los Pinos Creek near Saguache. The name was retained at the new site. At the time of the move, a sawmill was also brought in, the first in the Uncompahgre country, primarily to furnish lumber for the agency buildings.

The agency was a receiving and forwarding point for mail to and from Ouray and other San Juan mining camps. Although the agency was abandoned following the banishment of the Utes in 1881, it did not emerge as a town until after the building of the D & RG in 1886-87. The post office was established October 19, 1891. The 1896, Colorado Business Directory lists; "Colona, a small settlement and post office in Ouray County—population, 20."

The post office at Los Pinos Agency on the site of present-day Colona. About an equal admixture of Whites and Indians in this picture, probably agency personnel and some of their "customers."
(Colorado Historical Society)

Scene at Fort Crawford, the military cantonment on the Uncompahgre, four miles north of Los Pinos Agency. At far left is the hospital, left of center, the guard house and at far right, the bakery. One thousand soldiers were garrisoned at Fort Crawford, established in 1880. Although all the Utes were removed to Utah in 1881, the fort was not deactivated until 1890, long after there was any need for the soldiers' presence. Both the town and the county of Montrose were sorry to see the soldiers leave for they spent much of their paychecks in Montrose business establishments, and Uncle Sam was the county's biggest taxpayer. (Colorado Historical Society)

Nothing recognizable remains of Los Pinos Agency except the grave of George Beckwith, a post-rider stationed there, who was killed in a mixup of horses and lariat while trying to rope a fresh mount. He was a young man so his accomplishments may not yet have been many but he did establish the Colona cemetery.

Chief Ouray's farm and the Ute's permanent camp was eight miles further down the Uncompahgre Valley from the agency. There were usually Indians around the agency for one reason or another but on "issue day" the place really thronged with Indians. They came from all over the reservation, camped on the agency grounds and had themselves a great holiday. In summer, they scattered into the mountains to gather and dry fruits and herbs for winter use as well as to hunt and preserve game.

The Indians were friendly with the settlers to the south and would often travel to Ouray to compete in horse races with the whites near Dry Creek several miles south of the agency. Ernest Ingersoll, in 1883, reported that the abandoned agency was a stop for the stage and that the river was so close below the bluff "that water for the station-stables was drawn up by means of a pulley mounted in a tall scaffolding of poles standing in front of the cliff, and reached by a bridge. It was a 'well,' built some sixty feet out of ground."

The first deed in the area was given to the Denver & Rio Grande Railroad but no official patent for the land was issued until 1904. At one time, Colona had a brick plant, blacksmith, hotel, grocery store, post office, and several other stores. Cattle were shipped from the area and the train stopped twice a day.

The Colona Community Church has quite a history. The building was originally built in Ouray by the Methodist Church to the north across from the present-day Ouray Episcopal Church. It was hauled to Colona in

1912. Maybe "almost hauled" would be a better term as the freighter who hauled the church was supposedly drunk and unloaded the church four miles south of its correct location (local citizens finished the trip). The bell in the church was first used by the Denver Volunteer Fire Department and was donated to the Ouray Methodist Church in 1886 or 1887.

At Colona a dirt road leads to the east high up in the mountains to Buckhorn Lakes. There are two lakes - one large enough for boating. Both offer good fishing. The two lakes were once the water supply for the city of Montrose and are now a park. Camping sites are available although there are no facilities other than barbecue grills and a few outhouses.

Highway 550 follows the middle of the Uncompahgre Valley (mean altitude 5,000 feet) which is about thirty five miles long and an average of about twelve miles wide. The Uncompahgre River runs the entire length of the valley. Grand Mesa is visible to the north of the valley. To the west of the valley is Horsefly Mesa, then Spring Creek Mesa to the north. To the east is the Saw Tooth Range with its broken and ragged summit. The valley was used from early times for irrigated or "dry land" farming, first using the Uncompahgre River then the famous Gunnison Tunnel. Water shortages always appeared in late summer when the Uncompahgre River alone was used for irrigation. The Gunnison Tunnel was driven for six miles to bring the Gunnison River water to the valley.

Four miles north of Colona, on Highway 550, is the former site of Fort Crawford, or as it was originally called, "The Cantonment on the Uncompahgre." A "cantonment" was a temporary military fort or post or at least one intended to be temporary. The sign erected near the site by the State Historical Society of Colorado by the side of the highway tells the story well. It reads:

"Following the Meeker Massacre of 1879 and the ambush of Major T.T. Tornburgh's relief force, Colorado's residents demanded the removal of the Ute Indians. A treaty was signed, but the Uncompahgre Utes proved defiant, and in July 1880, the 'Cantonment on the Uncompahgre' was established to guard the settlers and pacify the Indians. After the Ute removal in 1881, the Camp settled down to routine garrison duty. In 1886, the post was renamed Fort Crawford in honor of Captain Emmet Crawford, killed that year fighting Geronimo's Apache band. By the end of the decade the fort had outlived its usefulness. It was deactivated in 1890. The buildings were sold at auction. The land was opened for settlement."

The reason the Utes had proved reluctant to move was that the local Uncompahgre Utes were forced into an agreement to go to Utah as a result of the Meeker massacre of September 29, 1879 (also called the White River Ute uprising). Meeker had taken charge of the agency in 1878 and immediately undertook to teach the Utes to be farmers instead of nomads. The Utes loved their free roaming ways and resisted his efforts. In the spring of 1879 the Ute began to scatter. When Meeker threatened to plow up their racetrack the Utes warned him he would be killed if he persisted. This frightened Meeker into sending for troops. The arrival of troops on the reservation land angered the Indians who attacked and killed Meeker and the other men at the agency. Since they had done nothing wrong, the local Utes saw no reason why they should be forced to move. However, the whites were looking for any excuse to get rid of the Indians and further feared a general uprising across the state. Ranald S. MacKenzie from Ft. Garland left May 18, 1880 and arrived May 25, 1880 with 15 companies of soldiers (six cavalry and nine infantry). On July 21, 1880, he established a "temporary" supply camp on the site on the west bank of the Uncompahgre and by late August a treaty had been negotiated with the Utes. They succeeded in keeping peace in the area and in August, a treaty agreeing to move to Utah was signed. MacKenzie withdrew, leaving Major Joshua and 250 men and officers to make the temporary camp into a permanent fort. The soldiers nearly froze to death that winter before getting permanent quarters built.

Colonel MacKenzie returned in the spring of 1881 with six companies of cavalry and four infantry, raising the Fort's population to over 1,000. When called on to move to Utah, the Uncompahgre Utes refused, and on August 23, 1881, the Indian commissioners (including Otto Mears) called upon the military to have them removed. Settlers were putting extreme pressure on the government to open the land that now constitutes Western Colorado. People started mining and occupying the land anyway. Otto Mears resorted to paying Indians $2.00 each if they would agree to move. On March 6, 1880 a treaty was signed. General John Pope, MacKenzie's commander wrote that the Utes "moved off in a day or two (after being threatened by force), but manifesting the greatest grief and regret at being obliged to abandon in this manner, the home of their tribe for so many years. The whites who had collected, in view of their removal, were so eager and so unrestrained by common decency that it was absolutely necessary to use military force to keep them off the reservation until the Indians were fairly gone." MacKenzie and the fourth cavalry left after the Ute's removal. Lt. Colonel Henry Douglass and four companies of infantry remained. However, social functions, hunting parties and beautifying the fort were their main activities. There was really no reason for the soldiers to stay, but the economy of the area would have suffered if they left (a problem still with us today). The post was abandoned December 30, 1890 and in early 1891, transferred south to the Department of the Interior. Now, only the tall cottonwoods, located behind the Historical Society sign and planted around the parade grounds remain.

About a mile south of Montrose is the Chief Ouray State Historical Monument and the Ute Indian Museum. At the time the Ute Indian Reservation was established on the Uncompahgre, the government built Ouray and Chipeta an adobe house. The house was furnished with beds, tables, chairs, rugs and stoves. The site of Chief Ouray's house was about one-eighth mile north of the site of the museum; no part of it is now standing though part of it, windowless and doorless was still there in the early 1930s. Ernest Ingersoll reported in 1885 that here

> "Ouray, the fine old head-chief of the Ute confederation, lived toward the end of his life in a good house built of adobe after the Mexican fashion, and cultivated neighboring bottom lands. His farm made the grand center of Ute interest, and from the pleasant groves near it radiated all the trails across mountain and plain. Many outhouses, of log and frame, surrounded the main building and testify

Chief Ouray's house near Montrose. Ouray's house stood for many years after his death and the banishment of his people, including his wife, Chipeta, from their ancient homeland—land that was guaranteed them by treaty "so long as rivers run and grasses grow." Only after the death of Chipeta in 1924 did compassionate, charitable white people become concerned about allowing Chief Ouray and Chipeta a final resting place on their own land. Chipeta is buried here but Indians in the Ignacio area, where Chief Ouray was buried, would not permit removal of his body to Montrose. (Colorado Historical Society)

Montrose Main Street, January 1924. It was just 42 years earlier (January 1882) that the first building was built in Montrose. Things moved along rapidly; the town was laid out in the same month and within another month's time, thirty buildings had been built or were in process of construction. The D&RG extended its tracks to Montrose before the end of the same year. (Colorado Historical Society)

that order was one of the great chief's good qualities. Here, after his death Chipeta (see **Widow of Ouray**), continued to live, raising farm products and pasturing sheep, and so attached had she become to the spot that she importuned the government to be granted the privilege of abandoning her race and returning to her farm home. The government refused this request, but decided to sell the farm for the personal benefit of Chipeta.''

Montrose was originally only a small watering stop for the railroad and a supply town for the surrounding area. The town was located by O.D. "Pappy" Loutsenhizer and Joseph Selig on January 20, 1882 (four months after the Utes left and nine months before the railroad arrived). Selig came from the town of Ruby in Gunnison County and found Loutsenhizer already in the area when he arrived. Loutsenhizer had been a member of the Alferd Packer party. The town was originally called Pomona. The first cabin was built in the first half of 1882 by a man named "Dad" Baird. David Lavender states the name was changed to Montrose to honor the Duchess of Montrose from **A Legend of Montrose**, a Sir Walter Scott novel. By the late part of February 1882, the town had been surveyed and platted. Montrose was definitely a railroad town - in fact most of the first buildings (which were built before the railroad came) were moved a half mile to be by the depot when it was built in the summer of 1882. The town was incorporated in April, 1882. By July, there were about 125 houses in the area where there had been but one at the first of the year. By 1905, the population was 3,000 with 800 school age children. A five room elementary school was being built and the brick high school was erected in 1904. The railroad construction caused its birth but it lasted after the crews were gone. Flour mills, lumber yards and hundreds of other "support" industries grew on the spot. After the Rio Grande Southern and Ouray branch of Denver and Rio Grande were built, the area became even more important as a junction point. In 1911, the old depot was replaced with the now existing structure. Today, Montrose is a fast-growing town of over 10,000.

Cascade Avenue, Montrose, May 1887. The town is now five years old. (Ruth Gregory Collection)

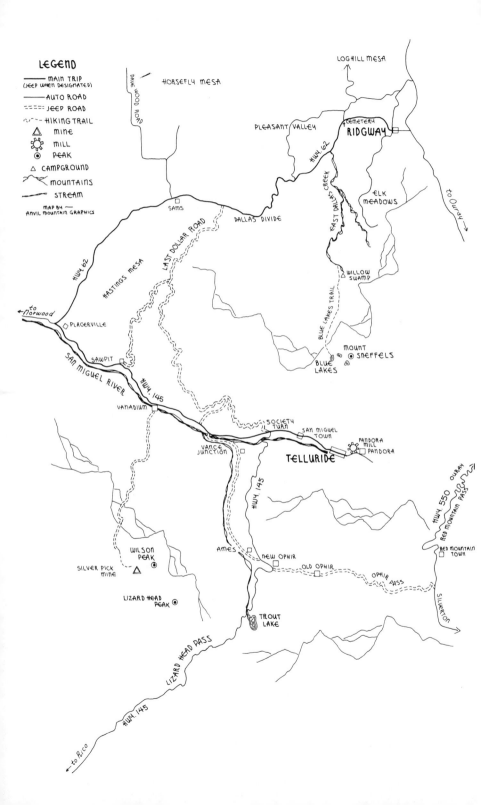

LOG HILL MESA

LEGEND

MAIN TRIP
(JEEP WHEN DESIGNATED)
AUTO ROAD
JEEP ROAD
HIKING TRAIL
△ MINE
✳ MILL
⊙ PEAK
△ CAMPGROUND
⏦ MOUNTAINS
⏦ STREAM

MAP BY
ANVIL MOUNTAIN GRAPHICS

HORSEFLY MESA

DAKEWOOD ROAD

PLEASANT VALLEY

RIDGWAY

CEMETERY

ELK MEADOWS

to Ouray

SAMS

DALLAS DIVIDE

HWY 62

HASTINGS MESA

LAST DOLLAR ROAD

EAST DALLAS CREEK

HWY 62

WILLOW SWAMP

BLUE LAKES TRAIL

to Norwood

PLACERVILLE

SAWPIT

SAN MIGUEL RIVER

HWY 145

VANADIUM

MOUNT SNEFFELS

BLUE LAKES

SOCIETY TURN

SAN MIGUEL TOWN

PANDORA MILL

PANDORA

VANCE JUNCTION

TELLURIDE

HWY 145

HWY 550

RED MOUNTAIN PASS

OURAY

WILSON PEAK

SILVER PICK MINE

LIZARD HEAD PEAK

AMES

NEW OPHIR

OLD OPHIR

OPHIR PASS

RED MOUNTAIN TOWN

SILVERTON

TROUT LAKE

LIZARD HEAD PASS

HWY 145

to Rico

CHAPTER 15
Ridgway to Telluride
Following Mears' Grand Detour

Ridgway, the child of the union of two railroads which was sustained by them for 50 years, has been covered in chapters 11 and 12. Therefore, we shall use it as the beginning point of yet another romantic, historic and scenic trip on which you may expend several hours or several days, depending upon whether you choose to take in some or all of the side trips on the many dirt roads that branch off the main paved highway. The trip follows Colorado 62, which begins at its junction with Highway 550 at Ridgway and ends at Placerville, where it joins Colorado 145.

Leaving the town of Ridgway at its west edge, we immediately climb out of the valley of the Uncompahgre, into another higher valley, down which flows Dallas Creek (also known by a not-so-uncommon but very appropriate name of "Pleasant Valley.") Two to three miles wide, Pleasant Valley is walled in on the north by Loghill Mesa and on the south by Miller Mesa and beyond that, the mighty Sneffels range. The range includes not only Mount Sneffels (14,150 feet) but also Potosi, Teakettle, Whitehouse, Gilpin and Mears. The Loghill area was traveled in 1776 by the 12-man Dominguez-Escalante expedition. Escalante was very impressed by the Sneffels range which he called Tabejuache Mountains or Sierra de Los Tabehuaches after the local Ute Indian bands. Loghill Mesa took its name from the fact of extensive logging in the area and a practice of teamsters that Jocknick described:

> "Freighters adopted the rough and ready device of hitching heavy log drags to their hind axletrees, letting them drag with their hind ends loose in the rear, after the manner of taking a cat by the tail, their spreading limbs acting like claws in clutching at all manner of temporary checks and thus delaying too rapid and pendulous descents. In the course of two seasons freighting down Loghill there were enough saw logs left on Dallas Creek to have set up a good sized sawmill in business."

For the first six or seven miles on either side of the highway are many small ranches primarily devoted to the raising of livestock and related activities. Shortly before Highway 62 crosses Dallas Creek, a dirt road to the left leads six miles high up toward Sneffels. Near the end of the road is Willow Swamp Campground. The area has fairly good (but hot and cold) fishing and by hiking five miles up the trail to Blue Lakes there is additionally good fishing (some very large fish) in all three lakes. Plan on a 3 to 4 hour hike each direction, or one can travel over the 13,000-foot pass and tie in with the trail in Yankee Boy basin.

Back on the main road (Highway 62), the final four miles of the eastern approach to the summit of Dallas Divide are the steepest (but not difficult); along this stretch, the "ranches" seem to become larger and are principally used for summer grazing. Dallas Divide, at only 8,970 feet above sea-level, is not high by Colorado standards, but has several other reasons for making a stop. There are plenty of wide areas for parking off the highway and it's flat enough that you won't be parking on a slope. Get out of the car, stretch your legs, quaff a few draughts of delicious, unpolluted, spruce-scented mountain air; look back in the direction from which you have just come. Visible besides the Sneffels range are Courthouse, Mountain, Chimney Rock, Matterhorn, Wetterhorn and Uncompahgre Peak, the highest of the San Juans at 14,309 feet. Also visible in the far distance are the Elk Mountains. (If the time of day and the light are right, you'll be glad you brought along extra film. You will also be glad that you didn't leave your telephoto lens behind).

Before continuing on from this Summit, study the terrain around you. Many signs of the railroad installations, the roadbed, loading chutes and switching tracks can still be made out. This is the first sign of the RGS since leaving Ridgway for the highway and railroad diverged there, using different approaches until both have gained the summit of Dallas Divide. In railroad days, there was a station and a post office at Dallas Divide.

Moving on from the divide another mile west, a dirt road branches to the left. The Last Dollar Road crosses high Hastings Mesa, the location of several early-day homesteads. All but one or two have been abandoned so far as year-round living and farming are concerned. The winters there were rigorous and the growing season too short for any crops except hay and short-season grain crops. This was an early mail and supply route to Telluride, in use before Otto Mears built the San Miguel canyon road.

"Fording" Dallas Divide in 1914. For those generations who have no memory of the "Model T," we should explain that it had no gearshift; it was automatic if the driver knew which of the three pedals to push and when to push 'em. It had two forward speeds, low and high. Low gear required holding the left pedal down hard with the left foot as long as that power ratio was needed. Putting 'er in high simply required removing one's foot from the left pedal. A hike from Ridgway up Dallas Divide would guarantee two very tired feet, while the same trip by Model T produced only one tired foot! (Ruth Gregory Collection)

Crossing, as it does, several large mountain parks, the feeling that comes over one is of vastness; even the sky seems bigger from there. Four-wheelers are recommended at the higher elevations but most cars could be driven over the lower part of Last Dollar except in wet weather. Six and one-half miles in on Hastings Mesa, the road forks. Taking the one to the right, we may travel down a mountainside shelf road and join

The tracks of the Rio Grande Southern, crossing a meadow in Pleasant Valley west of Ridgway. In the background, Mount Sneffels is in the center of the cluster of mountains. This is one of the most frequently photographed views in the region. The railroad tracks are no longer there. (Ruth Gregory Collection)

At the top of Dallas Divide, the Rio Grande Southern had a switching yard, cattle loading pens and water tank. There was, for a time, a post office called Dallas Divide, which was moved to Noel, a bit west of the summit. (Ruth Gregory Collection)

The store and post office at Sams, on the Rio Grande Southern (the tracks are behind the store, the highway in front). This was four miles down Leopard Creek on the western descent from Dallas Divide. A shelterhouse for a ski run (Ski Dallas) replaces the Sams store which burned after the abandonment of the railroad. (Ruth Gregory Collection)

Highway 145 at Sawpit. Stay to the left and we continue on across the mesa and join Colorado 145 at Society Turn, approximately four miles west of Telluride.

Four miles west of Dallas Divide we come to "Ski-Dallas," a shelterhouse and ski run with a T-bar lift. Since the larger development at Telluride, Ski-Dallas is not really in use any more. This was the site of "Sams," a station on the RGS with a store and post office, named after a conducter on the RGS. The store was still in operation as late as 1950, but as soon as service was discontinued on the RGS, Sams burned to the ground—contents and all! Sams just couldn't continue to exist without, at least, the services of the Galloping Goose!

Another station, 4.3 miles further down Leopard Creek, that was called a "small town" in railroad days, was Leonard. It was founded just after the close of the Spanish-American War at the end of the last century. In 1920, the population was 15 including "the Colorado Vanadium Mine Co., J. E. Gibson, General Merchandise, ice, postmaster; Miss Jane Gallagher, school principal; A.J. Hays, Lumber; W.S. Wolverton, general merchandise." So little evidence remains that it is scarely worth the stop. In fact, we're not even certain we could find it for you.

Continue down Leopard Creek to Placerville, the possessor of the second oldest post office in San Miguel County (established in 1878). The name, as you would naturally suppose, is the result of the discovery of placer deposits in the immediate area — a circumstance which always attracted prospectors and miners as flies are attracted to honey, and almost always resulted in the founding of a town. Here may still be seen great ridges of coarse rock, cast aside during large sluicing operations.

Placerville, 1887—three years before the coming of the railroad. The town was a natural division point for mail and coaches going toward Telluride, Ophir and Rico, or to Norwood, Nucla, Paradox and Gateway. As its name suggests, placer mining was the reason for its founding. (Colorado Historical Society)

Very large hydraulic operations were also carried on here, but by the time of the building of the Rio Grande Southern Railway, mining at the site was almost dead. The original location of the town was the junction of Leopard Creek and the San Miguel River. The town shifted to its present location where enough flat land was available for a depot and side tracks. The stock pens remained at "old town."

Placerville was a natural division point for mail and freight going either up the San Miguel River to Telluride and points beyond or down river to Norwood, thence to points in western San Miguel and Montrose counties and into eastern Utah. Here too, was the nearest and most practical loading point for the shipment of cattle from the Norwood, Paradox and Gateway areas. Many thousands of head of cattle were loaded at Placerville and started on their way to markets in the Midwest. Later, sheep became predominant, culminating in over 1,000 carloads being shipped in 1949.

Colorado 62 ends as it merges with Colorado 145 at Placerville. The present road (Colorado 145) follows the San Miguel River upstream sixteen miles to Telluride. The road basically follows the old railroad grade. A short way up-river from Placerville is the pretty little community called Fall Creek. It is situated on the north bank of the San Miguel, opposite the point where Fall Creek joins the river. Crossing the bridge, one may follow the road up that creek to Woods Lake, reputed to be a fine fishing spot and attainable by auto (at least in good weather). The little settlement of Fall Creek had a post office from 1933 to 1943. This place was originally called "Seymour" then "Silver Pick." A post office was established there in 1892, but was moved to Sawpit, a mile and a half farther east, in 1896.

Sawpit was originally named because of the trees cut in the area for placer mining. The trees were cut by John Donnellan and John Mitchell who used a large pit onto which logs were rolled with one man on top with one end of the hand saw and one man in the pit. The area boomed in 1895 when James Blake discovered the Champion Belle Mine whose first three carloads netted him $1,800. Men swarmed to the area. The 1896 Business Directory lists Sawpit as "a new mining town in San Miguel County 1½ miles west (an error for it is east) of Seymour, the nearest post office. Population 200." The 1920 directory gives a more lengthy description, but with the population reduced by one-half to 100. In March 1926, the post office was discontinued. In more recent times, the population has been as low as 25 but, being an incorporated town, they still have elections, electing a mayor and board of trustees. Sawpit, at least not long ago, claimed the distinction of being the best illuminated town, per unit of population, in the State of Colorado, having two gas-vapor street lights.

Yet a little farther eastward from Sawpit, a collection of old concrete foundations are at the side of the road. They constitute the remains of a vanadium processing mill. The place was originally called Newmire and a post office was established on April 4, 1895. The name was changed to Vanadium May 17, 1913, but the post office was discontinued in August of 1942. In 1920, the population was 350 and the industry was the mining

Cattle pens at Placerville. After the coming of the Rio Grande Southern Railway, Placerville became an important point for the shipment of livestock. It has been said that, in some years, more cattle were shipped out of Placerville than from any other place in Colorado. Vast cattle ranges were south, north and west of Norwood. The most economical way to get the cattle to market was to drive them to Placerville and ship them from there. (Ruth Gregory Collection)

and milling of vanadium, a valuable alloy used in the making of tough tool steel. Although it is usually combined with vanadium in carnotite ore, uranium was cast away onto the tailings for it had no market value at the time and very little was understood or known about radioactive materials. Nobody had dreamed of an atomic bomb or had any concern about radiation poisoning. At Vanadium to the south of the highway is another four-wheel-drive road that leads to the Silver Pick Mine on Wilson Peak. Do not misunderstand, Wilson Peak is not Mount Wilson. Neighbors, though they are, they are two different mountains. The Silver Pick is located at eight levels around 11,000 feet and produced over $750,000 in its time. There is also a lost gold mine tale about Mt. Wilson. The story goes that in the 1870s, two prospectors hit a very rich vein on its slopes, but they kept the exact location a secret. Then they disappeared. About ten years later, human bones, a cabin, rich ore and a sampling outfit were found in a small park high up on the mountain. But the mine couldn't be found!

Continuing on the highway, a short way farther east from Vanadium, we begin the long but not difficult grade up Keystone Hill. If you watch for it, only a short distance on the Keystone grade, a good dirt road leads off, again to the south (right). A sign with the word "Illium" marks the spot. This road is easily traveled by car and follows the south fork of the San Miguel River to Ophir, where it rejoins Highway 145. The trip may be used as part of a "loop," returning from Ophir to Telluride or continuing on to "Trout Lake, Lizard Head Pass, Rico, Dolores and Cortez.

The start leads us through a beautiful valley that offers many picture possibilities as well as a great deal of interesting history. A couple of miles after leaving the pavement is Vance Junction, the place where the spur track of the RGS to Telluride left the main line. Here, some of the coal-tipples still cling to the mountainside and an old railroad coach is rusting away near the coaling station. The coach served as an office until 1921 and was used as a register spot by the crews until the line was abandoned. The depot was a two-story building with a stationmaster and a post office some of the time (the post office was moved back and forth from Vance Junction to Illium, a half mile away). The train to Telluride left the main track at Vance Junction and traveled upstream to Illium where it followed a big loop to put it on the grade up Keystone Hill to Telluride.

Illium had its beginning as the site of the second hydroelectric power plant owned by the Telluride Power Company. the powerhouse buildings still remain at Illium but the generator, the pelton wheel and other power-making facilities have been dismantled and moved away. An eight-car spur, section house and wye were at the spot.

Another five miles brings us to Ames, originally a little mining and milling town, but its chief claim to fame is that it was the place where the world's first alternating current generating plant was built. It was also the first to generate and transmit alternating current over long distances for commercial purposes. Until that time, all existing generators, motors, lights or appliances were designed for direct current only, which could not be economically transmitted over long distances.

The plant at Ames was built in 1890 by L.L. Nunn, a Telluride lawyer and his brother P.N. Nunn, an engineer for the Gold King Mine, 2.6 miles away. It soon expanded its generating capabilities with the addition of the Illium plant and transmitted power to Telluride as well as to many of the mines in the region — even over Imogene Pass to serve the Camp Bird and the Revenue and other mines in the Sneffels district.

Within the same decade, many communities in the San Juan region had alternating current power systems. In 1913, the Western Colorado Power Company was formed, linking together most of the independent producers into a large network and thus reducing the cost of electricity to the users and making electric power available to many more. In still more recent times, the generating facilities of the Western Colorado Power Company have been absorbed by the still greater network of Colorado Ute Electric. The little hydroelectric plant at Ames — the one that started the whole business for the entire world — is still pumping kilowatts into the Colorado Ute system.

When the Rio Grande Southern was built, the tracks on the mountainside were four hundred feet above Ames. This caused the businesses and the post office to be moved a mile further upstream to New Ophir, leaving only the power plant and its operating personnel at the site. The present road passes at a considerable elevation above the Ames station, affording a bird's-eye view of the present generating plant at Ames.

At Ophir we rejoin Highway 145, and we must make a choice. Turn left and return to Telluride; turn right on the longer trip via Cortez, Durango and the Million Dollar Highway; or go straight and make the two miles up

"Old Ophir"—two miles up Howard's Fork, above the RGS railway's Ophir Loop where a newer settlement came to be known as "New Ophir." Ophir was founded in 1878, in what was then Ouray County. When San Miguel County was cut out of Ouray County in 1883, Ophir went along with the package. In the valley of Howard's Fork are some of the richest gold mines of early times. Also, probably no other region in the San Juans surpasses this valley for the number and magnitude of snow avalanches. Nor is the town itself immune to avalanche danger, as has been demonstrated in recent times. (Colorado Historical Society)

Howard's Fork to Old Ophir and over Ophir Pass to Chattanooga. The Ophir Pass Road is only nine miles long and is one of the easiest jeep roads in the area. The two miles to Old Ophir can be traveled by car. Ophir Pass was originally a toll road opened in 1881 as the main road from Silverton to Telluride. The pass peaks in rubble rock at 11,789 feet. Old Ophir was established in 1878 in what then was Ouray County, long before anyone dreamed that a railroad might be built through the country. Many large mines were located in the area. The area was originally called Howard's Fork after Lt. Howard who prospected the area in 1875. The name was later changed to the biblical city of riches. By 1879, over 400 mines were in the area. Later the town had its own water works, electric lights and stamp mills and arrastras for milling ore.

But in 1891, the Rio Grande Southern came steaming up the south fork of the San Miguel River and a fantastic bit of engineering was performed that came to be known as the "Ophir Loop" — a great loop, crossing the canyon and back again to gain elevation to put the train on the road to Trout Lake and Lizard Head Pass. Most businesses, the post office and many residents of Old Ophir moved two miles down the creek to be on the railroad. Naturally, the new community became known as "Ophir," but the old one continued to exist and became known as "Old Ophir."

At New Ophir was a depot and trackage to serve the Silver Bell Mill, as well as facilities for loading concentrates that arrived by aerial tramway from the mill at Alta, high in the mountains above the town. Before long, two saloons, a newspaper, several stores and a hotel were in the area.

Leaving New Ophir, turn right onto Highway 145. About one-half mile

The fabulous Ophir Loop on the Rio Grande Southern Railway at New Ophir. This was a fantastic piece of railroad engineering, such as has rarely been accomplished anywhere. Designed to get the trains out of the canyon of Howard's Fork and on their climb to Trout Lake and Lizard Head Pass, truly one of the wonders of mountain railroading. (Ruth Gregory Collection)

on the way back toward Telluride a dirt road branches to the right and may be followed to the old mining camp of Alta. Here are the ghost-remains of a once lively mining camp. It never made any claim to being a "town" and it never had a post office, but it made up a sizeable community nevertheless. The Alta Mine was the main one in the area on Silver Mountain. Fossett reported that it had mill runs of 265 and 290 ounces of silver per ton. A boardinghouse, school, cabins and a 40 stamp mill were in the area. The Gold King Mine was in the same basin. The first ten sacks of ore from the mine brought $5,000. By 1890, the Gold King produced $200,000 per year. Nearby is a cluster of three small mountain lakes, known, of course, as the "Alta Lakes." Fishing must be good for we have rarely passed the place in the summer months when fishermen were not present. From Alta, an old road known as the "Boomerang Road" (not by any means suitable for cars — four-wheelers only) winds its way down through rich forest and rough terrain, coming out of the mountains to join Highway 145 at the site of the former town of San Miguel, two miles west of Telluride.

Further Reading

ARMSTRONG, Betsy R. and Richard L., **Avalanche Hazard in Ouray County, Colorado**, Institute of Arctic and Alpine Research, University of Colo., Boulder, Colorado, 1977

Avalanche Atlas, Ouray County, Colorado, Institute of Arctic and Alpine Research, University of Colorado, Silverton, 1977

A History of Avalanche Hazard in San Juan County, Colorado, Boulder, Colorado, the Regents of the University of Colorado, 1976

ARMSTRONG, Richard L. and Ives, Jack D., Editors, **Avalanche Releases and Snow Characteristics—San Juan Mountains**, University of Colorado at Boulder Press, 1976

BACKUS, Harriet Fish, **Tomboy Bride**, Pruett Press, Boulder, Colorado, 1969

BANCROFT, Caroline, **Colorful Colorado: Its Dramatic History**, Pruett Press, Boulder, Colorado, 1959

Unique Ghost Towns, Johnson Publishing Co., Boulder, Colorado, 1967

BATES, Margaret A., **A Quick History of Lake City, Colorado**, Little London Press, Colorado Springs, Colorado, 1973

BAUER, W.H., Ozment, J.L. and Willard, J.H., **Colorado Postal History**, J.B. Publishing Co., Crete, Nebraska, 1971

BENHAM, J.L., **Camp Bird and the Revenue**, Bear Creek Publishing Co., Ouray, Colorado 1980

Ouray, Bear Creek Publishing Co., Ouray, Colorado, 1976

Silverton and Neighboring Ghost Towns, Bear Creek Publishing Co., Ouray, Colorado, 1977

Colorado Railroad Museum, (various authors) **The Collected Colorado Railroad Annual**, (particularly nos. 9, 11 and 14), Colorado Railroad Museum, Golden, Colorado

CROFUTT, George, **Crofutt's Gripsack Guide of Colorado**, The Overland Publishing Co., Omaha, Nebraska, 1885

CROUTER, George A., **Colorado's Highest**, Sundance Publications, Ltd., Silverton, Colorado, 1977

CRUM, Josie Moore, **Three Little Lines**, Durango Herald News, Durango, Colorado, 1960

The Rio Grande Southern Railroad, 1961, Durango San Juan History, Inc. (publishers) Hamilton Press, Inc. (printers)

DALLAS, Sandra, **No More Than Five in a Bed**, University of Oklahoma Press, Norman, Oklahoma, 1967

DARLEY, Rev. George A., **Pioneering in the San Juan**, Fleming H. Revel Co., Chicago, 1899

FOSSETT, Frank, **Colorado, Its Gold and Silver Mines**, N.Y., C.G. Crawford, 1880

GANTT, Paul H., **The Case of Alferd Packer**, University of Denver Press, 1952

GIBBONS, Rev. J.J., **In the San Juan Colorado**, Calumet Book & Engraving Co., Chicago, 1898

GRIFFITHS, Thomas M., **San Juan Country**, Pruett Publishing Co., Boulder, Colorado, 1984

GRISWOLD, Don and Jean; Fred and Jo Mazulla, **Colorado's Century of "Cities,"** Smith-Brooks Printing Co., 1958

HALL, C.L., **Resources, Industries and Advantages of Ouray County, Colorado**

JOCKNICK, Sidney, **Early Days on the Western Slope of Colorado**, The Rio Grande Press, Glorietta, New Mexico, 1913

KAPLAN, Michael, **Otto Mears, Paradoxical Pathfinder**, San Juan County Book Co., Silverton Standard (printers), Allen Nossaman (editor)

KUSHNER, Ervan F., **Otto Mears: His Life and Times**, Jende-Hagen Bookcorp, Frederick, Colorado, 1979

LAVENDER, David, **One Man's West**, Doubleday-Doran, 1943

Colorado, Doubleday & Co., Inc., Garden City, N.Y., 1976

Red Mountain, Doubleday & Co., Inc.

The Rockies, Harper & Row, 1968

LIVERMORE, Robert, **Bostonians and Buillion**, University of Nebraska Press, Lincoln, Nebraska, 1968

MANGAN, **Colorado on Glass**, Sundance Publications, Ltd., 1975

McLEAN, Evalyn Walsh, **Father Struck it Rich**, 1936, Little Brown & Co., Boston, Massachusetts

ORMES, Robert M., **Guide to the Colorado Mountains**, Sage Books, 1973 (revised edition)

OURAY COUNTY PLAINDEALER, **Ouray Centennial-Historic Issue**, Ouray, Colorado, 1976

RATHMELL, Ruth, **Of Record and Reminiscence**, Ouray County Plaindealer and Herald, 1976

RICE, Frank A., **A History of Ouray and Ouray County**, Unpublished Manuscript, (Ouray Public Library)

RICKARD, T.A., **Across the San Juan Mountains**, 1907, Republished by Bear Creek Publishing, Ouray, Colorado, 1980

ROCKWELL, Wilson, **The Utes—A Forgotten People**, Sage Books, Denver, Colorado, 1956

Sunset Slope, 1956, Big Mountain Press, Denver, Colorado

Uncompahgre Country, 1965, Sage Books, Denver, Colorado

SMITH, Duane A., **Song of the Hammer and Drill**, 1982, Colorado School of Mines Press

Colorado Mining, University of New Mexico Press, 1977

Rocky Mountain Mining Camps, The Urban Frontier, 1967, University of Nebraska Press, Lincoln, Nebraska

SMITH, P. David, **Ouray - Chief of the Utes**, 1986, Wayfinder Press, Ouray, Colorado

SMITH-GREGORY, **The Million Dollar Highway**, 1986, Wayfinder Press, Ouray, Colorado

SMITH-VANDENBUSCH, **A Land Alone**, 1981, Pruett Publishing Co., Boulder, Colorado

SLOAN, Robert E. and Skowronski, Carl A., **The Rainbow Route**, 1975, Sundance Publications, Ltd., Denver, Colorado

UBBELOHDE, Carl; Maxine Benson; Duane A. Smith, **A Colorado History**, 1976, Pruett Publishing Co., Boulder

VANDENBUSCH, **Early Days in Gunnison Country**, 1974, B & B Printers, Gunnison, Colorado

WOLLE, Muriel Sibelle, **Timberline Tailings**, 1977, Swallow Press, Chicago, Illinois

Stampede to Timberline, 1949, Swallow Press, Chicago, Illinois, 1977

WOOD, Dorothy and Frances, **I Hauled These Mountains in Here**, 1977, Caxton Printers, Ltd., Caldwell, Idaho

Index

Field Notes

Field Notes

Field Notes

Field Notes

Field Notes

Field Notes